COMMONSENSE
SPECULATION

COMMONSENSE SPECULATION

by

"The Trader"

FRASER PUBLISHING COMPANY
Burlington, Vermont

Originally published in 1938 by
BARRON'S PUBLISHING COMPANY

Copyright ©1992 Fraser Publishing Company
a division of
Fraser Management Associates
Box 494
Burlington, VT 05402

Library of Congress Catalog Card Number: 92-71284

ISBN: 0-87034-103-0

Printed in the United States of America

FOREWORD

BECAUSE investment is really involuntary speculation, because speculation itself appears to be as
legitimate as any form of risk-taking business activity,
and, finally, because there are no omnipotent "they"
who depress or elevate prices, these observations, based on
twenty-five years study of the factors that influence the
trend of the stock market, are offered in the hope that they
will aid the average investor-speculator to make better
use of his capital and opportunities.

The Trader

INTRODUCTION

COMMONSENSE SPECULATION brings together in one compact volume the cream of nearly two decades of stock market lore.

Written by the author of the internationally famous column, THE TRADER VIEWS THE MARKET, in *Barron's, The National Financial Weekly*, this volume already has been reserved No. 1 position on the bookshelves of hundreds of business men and investors as a result of its serial publication in *Barron's*.

The ideas, anecdotes and counsel bound within these covers are the outpourings of no academic mind, nor of a flash-in-the-pan gambler, but of a shrewd New Englander who for 17 years has been carving out for himself a unique niche among financial writers as a commentator on the American economic scene. Yankee by birth and education, he has steadfastly refused to be lured permanently into Wall Street. Yet by dint of long distance telephoning and much flying, he keeps in as close touch with the men whose opinions he values in New York, Chicago, Detroit—and at times, Florida—as though he were quadruplets living in all four places.

Probably every man who reads this can recall at least one good hunch he has had about the market. How many would care to have all of their views of the market for nearly 20 years on file in cold type for comparison with what subsequently happened? The fact that The Trader, through his weekly column in *Barron's*, has his present eager following after years and years of daring to say what he thought of the market tells its own story.

When we say eager following, that's just what we mean. The Trader's views go by air mail weekly to points as far distant as the Dutch East Indies. They are flashed across the American continent by direct wires, "traveling" first class just like the hottest news. Why? What can The Trader do that everyone else can't do? What's his secret?

Remember the story of the business man and the statistician riding on the train together through the sheep country out west?

"Seventy-seven sheep in that flock," remarked the statistician as they whistled by.

"Whew!" said the business man, "how could you tell?"

"Easy," replied the statistician, "I just counted their legs and divided by four."

Wall Street probably has more than its share of people who count sheep that way. The Trader, as we suggested before, is not one of them. No magic formulae for him, no charts, no moving averages, no higher mathematics. First and last, he's an inquiring reporter—open-minded, flexible, inquisitive, ubiquitous and skeptical. Add to that the fact that the leaders of industry and finance are now as eager to check their views against his as he is to see them, and you have—The Trader.

That doesn't mean that he has never been wrong. The Oracle of Delphi was never wrong, but The Trader is not oracular. On the contrary, early in 1937 his comments on the dangers in the stock market were so forthright that one irate young bull speculator wrote to the Editor of *Barron's* canceling his subscription "until The Trader gets back on the track."

His flexibility of mind is one of The Trader's greatest assets. He learned, long ago, that pride of opinion is the most expensive and least satisfying of vices. While he can stick to his guns under the heaviest bombardment of "dud" shells, let one loaded with new facts burst near him and he will abandon his position before the fragments hit the ground.

He has, of course, the essential dash of cynicism. One of his favorite stories is the analogy of the stock market to the old parlor game called "Musical Chairs", related by Clifford B. Reeves in The Atlantic Monthly recently. As Reeves told it, "Someone plays a piano and everyone else walks around a double row of chairs, placed back-to-back. When there is no need to sit in them, it looks as though there were plenty of chairs. But when the music stops and everyone scrambles for a seat, there aren't enough chairs to go round. Someone always gets left out.

"A market is just the same. When you and millions of other people walk around with a few stock certificates you don't want to sell, you read of the bids being made for your stocks, and there seem to be plenty. But when the sweet music of good news stops, and you all try to sell at the same time, you find that there aren't enough bids to go around—except perhaps at shocking concessions in price."

The book that follows was not originally The Trader's idea. He would tell you if you asked him that there isn't a thing in it that you don't already know. You can take it from those who have read it that all unconsciously he would be paying you a high compliment when he said so.

Like Herman Melville's *White Jacket*, The Trader has been 17 years "serenely concocting information into wisdom." "Serenely" is part of the quotation and somehow doesn't fit The Trader. The rest of it, though, we think you'll agree, has Commonsense Speculation down pat.

T. W. P.

CONTENTS

CONTENTS

CHAPTER ONE

Legitimacy of Speculation

A Reasoned Anticipation of Future Conditions—
All Life Full of Hazards—No Investment Remains
Static—Bernard Baruch's Rules

"IN this world nothing is certain but death and taxes." Benjamin Franklin penned this adage in 1789. It was long before the factory age and the rise of industrialism in England. It was a century before the trust movement of the late '90s brought into being the bulk of the major American corporations of today, the securities of which are listed on the New York Stock Exchange. In a world threatened more and more by war and harassed by increasing taxes, the eternal truth of Poor Richard's adage must constantly be kept in mind by every individual with capital to protect.

The trend of governmental actions the world over, and particularly in the United States, is undoubtedly in the direction of a managed economy. As a result, it is widely maintained that, with the New Deal in the saddle, it is virtually a waste of time to apply orthodox rules in the determination of an investment attitude. "Sooner or later the tax collector will get you" is the plaint. All this is the complete philosophy of defeatism. In investing, as in everything else, one has to deal with conditions as they exist.

The laissez-faire investment policy resolves itself into the purchase of "governments", the maintenance of a strong cash position or the selection of a diversified portfolio of the strongest equities. "Governments" and cash are virtually the same. The theory of acquiring representative equities is that if the stocks of the soundest and best managed corporations have no future, then government itself is headed for the rocks. But a "do-nothing" policy is one that few and certainly no alert investors can afford to adopt.

For all the latter-day restrictions, speculation is still functioning in the two great English-speaking nations of the world. To be sure, the rules are different. Taxes sharply penalize the rewards of diligence and shrewdness. The regulations of the Securities and Exchange Commission, too, have made impossible the coups and quick fortunes of the past. Yet Wall Street is still the outstanding marketplace of the world—a free and open arena for security operations—where, now that the abuses and deceptions of manipulation have been outlawed, no one can honestly claim that the cards are stacked against him.

Speculation is an ingrained human quality. As deep-seated is it as the craving for alcohol, which Prohibition could not legislate out of existence. Reforms usually go too far. The further SEC regulation goes in fettering the market, the nearer draws the day of change.

As Clifford B. Reeves says in the May, 1938, issue of *The Atlantic Monthly* . . . "zeal for reform should not blind anyone to the fact that the securities markets perform an indispensable function in the present economic structure, by keeping vast amounts of capital liquid, mobile, and dynamic. When regulation, restriction, taxation, or any other measures result in the failure of markets to perform their proper functions in providing liquidity at fair values, then reform defeats its own purposes. . . . Improperly restricted markets can be a great menace to economic equilibrium and a serious deterrent to new capital investment and economic growth."

The human desire to make money and to assume risks in so doing is demonstrated by the fact that where the stock market is a minor national element, gambling of some sort evolves— horse racing in England, casinos in France and lotteries in Spain. Note the enormous increase in gambling right here in the United States. In a depression year the Florida State Racing Association reports an attendance during the 1937-38 season of 2,401,378 persons at horse races, dog races and jai alai games. The number of persons represented an increase of 70,434 over the 1936-37 season, and wagering was nearly $4,000,000 greater at the amazing figure of $54,047,114.

The distinction between speculation and gambling was never better drawn than by Winthrop W. Aldrich, chairman of the Chase National Bank, in his address on Oct. 14, 1937, before the Rochester, N. Y., Chamber of Commerce:

"I know that the whole system of speculation in securities is questioned by some; that speculation, as a whole, in any market is condemned by some; I know that there are those who identify all speculation with gambling, and who would rule out all speculators as social parasites who have no useful function. But the verdict of impartial economists on this point is clear and very nearly unanimous. The difference between speculation and gambling is that in gambling artificial and unnecessary risks are created, whereas in speculation the risks already exist and the question is simply who shall bear them.

"There is no reason why any financial result at all should depend on the throwing of dice except as men agree that a financial consequence should result therefrom. But, whether we like it or not, whether we agree or not, real and important financial consequences do hinge on a change in price, whether of commodities or of securities. Such changes in prices will inevitably occur for a great variety of reasons. The risk of a price change is there, whether we like it or not.

"Now, the speculator is a risk bearer. He takes a risk which somebody else wishes to get rid of. And he takes it because he thinks he can make a profit by so doing. He is not a philanthropist; he is a money maker, or hopes to be. He is a successful speculator to the extent that his judgment as to the nature of the risk is good judgment.

"To the extent that speculation is informed, to the extent that speculators trade within the limit of their ability to bear risks, to the extent that stock transactions are carried on by men of knowledge and experience and courage, the stock market is made safer, the whole body of investors is made safer, the collection of funds for industrial use from a wide body of people is made safer and easier, and our general economic life is served."

Despite the well warranted criticism of the abuses of the 1924-29 boom, stock market speculation requires no economic defense. The tendency in all depressions is to blame the stock market for the collapse of business. Such a view makes about as much sense as ascribing a cold wave to a fall in temperature. The stock market merely registers, and does not *cause*, what takes place in the realm of business and profits.

No stock can remain more static than life itself, which is full of change and hazards. Human beings grow from infancy to maturity, decline into old age and die. It is the same over the years with various forms of industry. Speculation merely attempts to anticipate the inevitabilities of future changing conditions.

Generations ago canal and toll bridge stocks were gilt-edged investments. In due course both were destroyed by the workings of time and obsolescence. By now speculative dodoes, street railway stocks early this century were prime investments. In the days of Theodore Roosevelt railroad shares were the investment-elect. Under Franklin D. Roosevelt rail equities have almost disappeared. In the boom of a decade ago the public utilities ranked highest. Now utilities are politically friendless. Amply disproved by now is belief in permanent popularity of any class of stocks.

That is why deathbed investment advice is so dangerous. Usually it is an injunction never to sell such-and-such a stock. But no one can look far ahead. To their unhappiness, New Englanders can recall the collapse of New Haven and the deterioration of American Sugar. Westerners have had equally discomfiting experiences with the receivershipped St. Paul and the old "Hill roads", Northern Pacific and Great Northern.

The fact is that a perfect investment has yet to be discovered. In the opinion of the writer the nearest approach is probably United Shoe Machinery, which is a benevolent monopoly of machinery necessary for the manufacture of an elemental human need. Yet, who can say what could happen to benevolent monopolies, buttressed by patent rights, if the Administration's anti-monopolistic crusade were carried beyond reasonable business bounds? Even a sound investment is susceptible to a sickening market decline, as witness the drop in United Shoe common to 50, from 98, in the period from January, 1937 to March, 1938.

When Governments repudiate pledges to repay obligations in gold, when the gold standard itself is abandoned, when governmental bonds have depreciated—as they have in Russia, Germany, France, South America and elsewhere—who can say what is an airtight, permanent investment? At times even national currencies have fluctuated more violently than stocks.

The legitimacy of speculation and its vital part in the financial welfare of individuals ought to be clear. Speculative funds are neither "hot" money nor "mad" money. Intelligently exercised, speculation is not gambling, but a reasoned attempt to anticipate a future condition or set of circumstances. The Websterian definition of speculation says: "Speculation, while confined within moderate limits, is the agent for equalizing supply and demand, and rendering the fluctuations of price less sudden and abrupt than they would otherwise be."

Unwillingness or inability of bankers and business men, preoccupied with the affairs of the moment, to visualize a sudden change for the worse or better some months hence is what makes poor speculators of those who should be the best. The main reason why speculative leaders have enjoyed little caste is that they tend to overdo a movement.

W. C. Durant, long the head of General Motors, and a famous Wall Street bull, is a case in point. An inveterate optimist, Durant, after pushing General Motors to dizzy heights, made the further mistake of attempting to support a falling market in 1921.

A sharp break or advance in the quotation of a stock brings it into clear relief. Stockholders immediately become aware that something is happening. If the break or the advance fails to hold over a period, then the movement is probably a flash in the pan. If it is extended, it is usually significant.

Back in 1930 Gillette Safety Razor regarded as an A1+ investment which had previously been normally selling well over $100 a share drifted into the 90s and then suddenly broke $6 in a single session into the 80's. A member of the executive committee had his attention called to the development by his secretary who had noted the quotation on the financial news service. The director studied the price for some minutes and exclaimed: "There is certainly something wrong here, but I'll be hanged if I know what it is!" Not until months later were the deceptive accounting practices revealed. Abrupt price changes like the ominous decline in Gillette are usually definitely symptomatic of important pending developments.

First indication of "breakers ahead" for business was the stock market collapse of September, 1937. Industrial production, sales and employment indexes were all favorable. But the stock market, with its unerring diagnosis, had uncovered the sore of swollen inventories. Industrialists were prone at first to minimize the significance of the shrinkage of billions in market values of securities, but lost no time in cancelling forward commitments and capital outlays. Six months later the message of the market was clear to the most rabid New Dealer.

Concerning capital, people are proverbially careless. In boom times the human ego is such that big gains are ascribed to unique, individual judgment. The truth is that they are the product of a tidal movement. Again, in hard times, a "drifting" policy also prevails. Mistakes—properly to be placed on conceit or on a naïve belief in America as an El Dorado—are blamed on politicians. With respect to protection of investment capital, human beings seem to display more laziness than in any other important field of activity.

From laziness and fear has come the great growth in life insurance. Committed to a fixed insurance charge, the small or medium-sized capitalist figures that his capital responsibilities are terminated. While insurance is an indispensable protection and a saving, the return on capital is extremely small. For the wealthy there is from insurance a concealed return in the form of tax saving on investment that yields no reportable income. But, fundamentally, carrying an excessive amount of insurance represents the delegation of financial responsibility. The more financial responsibility is delegated, the less essential knowledge of finance there is bound to be on the part of the individual.

To become reasonably adept in handling capital should be as much a part of everyday education as the keeping of a checkbook now. To become proficient in the art of speculation involves initiative and intensive study. Though a man-sized task, it is by no means insoluble. The soothsayers in high places do not necessarily understand it. The collapse of 1929-32 has erased the glamour that used to be attached to the utterances of so-called industrial and banking giants. Investment trust managers revealed no "sixth sense" in 1936 or 1937. There is no magic formula of speculative success. The first step toward success is an open and realistically curious approach.

After all, there should be willingness to spend time and study on a vital problem that involves so little in the way of physical labor. The only hard work a speculator does is to make a decision. Once made, all he has to do is to telephone an order to a banker or broker who handles every detail of the transaction.

Contrast that simple procedure with all the sweat and worry which a managing executive undergoes. Business has to acquire raw materials, fabricate them into finished goods with the aid of machinery and labor, sell the goods, collect the bills, determine the profit—if any—pay the taxes, and, finally, distribute the dividends.

A falling market may be hard on the nerves of a speculator, but his travail is far less than that suffered by corporate executives in a business depression. For anything so simply done as the buying and selling of securities, there must obviously be the compensatory recurrent periods of mental strain.

General Hugh S. Johnson quoted Bernard M. Baruch, of whom he relates there never was any more successful speculator, as saying: "Buying and paying outright for a stock because it pays an income and because careful expert study shows that it is highly likely to continue is like buying a dry-goods store. All business is a hazard." Likening the purchase of a stock to the acquisition of a dry-goods store, which must face the style and price problems of myriad items of merchandise, emphasizes the hazards ever-present in all stocks.

More penetrating is the Baruch advice on the requisites for successful speculation. The quotation below, also from General Johnson, gives some idea of the application and tenacity required to come out on top. "If you are ready and able to give up every-thing else—to study the whole history and background of the market and all of the principal companies whose stocks are on the board as carefully as a medical student studies anatomy—to glue your nose to the tape at the opening of every day of the year and never take it off until night—if you can do all that, and, in addi-tion, you have the cool nerves of a great gambler, the sixth sense of a kind of clairvoyant, and the courage of the lion, you have a Chinaman's chance."

A trifle discouraging all this may be to the average busy man, but more admonitory than repressive is its implication. For history repeats itself and out of close-range observations of the fluctuations of the stock market over the years can be gleaned certain commonsense ideas that may be *at least* valuable in combating emotional and careless investment thinking.

CHAPTER TWO

"Sell on the First Margin Call"

Borrowing Makes for Alertness—Stocks Worth
Only What They Sell For—Dangers of Mass
Psychology—Earning Power All-Important

STOCK market speculation, in the public mind, connotes
marginal operations, and marginal trading has always been
regarded as almost akin to moral turpitude. Among the self-
righteous the marginal stock trader is viewed as being financially
irresponsible—a shoe-string gambler. The crystallized aversion
to marginal trading undoubtedly has come about from the
thousands of people ruined by shakeouts in bull markets or by
prolonged bear markets, where proverbial "lifetime savings"
frequently have been lost.

The constitutional distaste for borrowing on stocks seems
decidedly ill-founded. It has been the experience of the writer
that just as much money has been lost in outright-owned commitments. Over and over again, amateur speculators and investors
have averred, "Well, I own my stocks outright, so I have nothing
to worry about." If, however, there is some borrowing on the
part of the speculator, he becomes much more alert—much more
alive to price movements and financial developments—and he is
much less likely to stand by idly as his capital dwindles.

Outright ownership too often makes for flabby reasoning
and a sense of false security. The original heavy marginal
requirements enforced by the SEC were partially responsible for
the October debacle. Hundreds of people in 1937 figured that,
with a 55% margin, not even a panic could bring them into
difficulty.

In the pre-SEC days of 10% margins there used to be a
cynical axiom, said to have been coined by a hardboiled margin

clerk, "Always sell on the first margin call." What that meant
was that an initial break, sufficient to impair a margin, in nine
cases out of 10 represented the first leg of a serious downward
movement that called for prompt liquidation instead of bolstering
of accounts. While a great many people failed to follow such
cynical advice, nevertheless slight margins—as in the case of
1929—saved many speculators from putting good money up after
bad. Last fall, for all our heavy margins, the panic—that was
supposed to have been legislated out of existence—came with
appalling severity and suddenness and wiped out hundreds of
accounts that 60 days earlier had seemed impregnable.

There is nothing nefarious per se about borrowing on securities any more than there is in commercial borrowing. How
do all corporate bonds, which represent borrowing, come into
existence, unless the companies can see a return from the investment greater than the interest paid out? The elder John D.
Rockefeller used to advise all young men to go into debt up
to their necks if they knew what they were doing and had a
proper outlet for the funds. The debt, Rockefeller maintained,
should be paid off in later life.

United Fruit Co., now a financial Rock of Gibraltar, was a
recurrent borrower 25 or 30 years ago during the big period of
expansion. Invariably every fresh note or bond or stock issue
would be followed by a decline in the stock. Veteran President
Andrew W. Preston, who lived to see the day when the company had a single-class stock with no securities ahead of it, used
to say that he had to avoid friends when the stock broke on the
news of new borrowing. But Preston had the vision which short-
sighted speculators, fearful of borrowing, lacked.

More to the point, Chrysler Corp. on May 1, 1935, paid
off the entire Dodge Brothers, Inc., 6% bond issue which it
had inherited with the 1928 purchase, taking advantage of the
extreme money ease to refund through one, two, three, four and
five-year loans. By June 15 of the following year, with the aid of
huge earnings, it had retired its entire line of bank loans. Now,
if a man had simply followed along, by purchasing Chrysler when

the company's directors showed their confidence in the immediate future of earnings by converting a long-term bond issue into short-term loans, and sold when the company decided to pay off the loans before it was necessary, he would have got in around 38 and out around 98. A speculator operating on a 55% margin would have almost trebled his capital in some 13 months.

Obviously, if marginal operations are to be undertaken, the chances for the profitable employment of borrowed funds are infinitely greater and the risks are infinitely smaller at the bottom of a long market decline. Reasonably small at that time is the possibility of a sudden break necessitating forced selling. It is the fear of a rapid erosion of values that produces mental travail. Constant worry over being sold out is what preys on the marginal operator. The best start, then, for marginal buying is at the bottom of a bear market.

If an investor can buy stocks after a serious decline, with some assurance, therefore, that in a year or two the capital appreciation or enhanced dividends will wipe out interest charges, then marginal buying can hardly be deemed foolhardy. Marginal buying is commonly blamed for the disasters wholly attributable to buying at the wrong time.

Along with the aversion to marginal trading there used to exist an inherent distrust of stock brokers and their advices. The feeling grew up in the loose days of indiscriminate "tipping" and high-pressure solicitation by customers men, greedy for commissions. Stock brokerage today is a chastened and reformed business. It has to operate under the strictest of rules. There are no pools to fool the guileless, and no secret commissions. Everything is out in the open. Hit-or-miss opinions are dangerous. The conscientious and aggressive stock broker of today must, perforce, be an up-to-date investment counselor.

To take a leaf out of brokers' books, the stark truth always to be recognized by a speculator is that stocks listed on the New York Stock Exchange are worth only what they command every night at the close of dealings. Of course the Stock Exchange sets the trend for all other issues. Exactly the levels at which stocks are valued by margin clerks or collateral loan clerks are all they really are worth.

Opinions of their near-term or long-term trend may vary, a price upheaval may at any time be in the making, but the prices on the New York Stock Exchange are the real and only true determinant of the net worth of listed security portfolios of individuals or institutions. The preservation of a strict accounting attitude toward stock quotations is the first lesson to be digested by every investor-speculator.

The investor or speculator should audit his books—or at least take soundings—oftener than a corporation does. Even though a business enterprise audits its books only once a year, it has sufficient control and knowledge of inventories and other costs to make a close approximation of its profits or losses from month to month. Proper gearing of manufacturing and selling operations requires a business to know from month to month, if not from week to week, just how it is faring and whence it is heading. The investor must copy the technique of the business man.

But investors en masse are likely, in giving superficial attention to their most vital problem, the preservation of capital, to analyze their holdings only after a drastic change in prices. Even then, the tendency is to delay the detailed examination until a new set of conditions has become so glaring as to be first-page news or everyday conversation. By the time the status of the market, as a whole, or of an individual security is radically altered, the damage has been done. Just as with sickness, "an ounce of prevention is worth a pound of cure" for investment capital.

No stock can be neglected. None can be put away and forgotten. Every single issue ought to be regarded by its owner as a hot potato to be dropped some time or other.

Eternal vigilance is the only rule for investment success. The care of capital involves fully as much attention as the human body, a house, or a car, for instance. It is not sufficient to review holdings quarterly or semi-annually, or annually. Investments must be studied all the time for signs of deterioration or growth.

One good rule of thumb is to ask oneself, if there is a reluctance to sell, whether there is not an equal aversion to buy. If there isn't warrant for buying a stock after a big appreciation, the chances are it ought to be sold. *It is the market price, not the original purchase price, that must govern the decision.*

One of the commonest of speculative sins is to be unduly influenced by the previous high of a stock. If the price has declined a good many points, a universal failing is to assume that it cannot go much lower. The stock market can do anything and an individual stock can go almost anywhere—up or down—in the course of a dynamic move.

A period of rising or high prices breeds the greatest carelessness on the part of the rank and file of security holders. Any broker or financial newspaper can testify that almost never is here then a request for advice as to whether a profit should be taken. That is when the human ego, asserting itself, concludes that the capital appreciation came about from the exercise of innate shrewdness and not from a broad tidal movement. When stocks are high the certainty of an ultimate ebbing of the tide is commonly forgotten.

Yet it is just as important to look portfolios over when the skies are clear as when trouble is in the wind or a depression in the offing. The hoariest of advice is "No one ever went broke taking profits." In extravagant bull markets the pendulum always swings so high as to force certain groups of stocks, as utilities in 1929, far above long-term values. When mass enthusiasm runs highest is when investment skepticism, instead of self-satisfaction, should be greatest.

The "patter" of the marketplace is likely to make for confusion. Financial writers of all sorts, obliged by their calling to purvey daily advices, tend to employ phrases that, by their repetition, weave a philosophy demoralizing to the easy-going or unastute investor. The foolish 1920's evolved the naïve belief that mass production had created a limitless prosperity. Those were the days of "two automobiles in every garage." With the New Deal came the fetish of inflation which rejected the notion that cash could have lasting value and espoused the idea that commodities, equities and even real estate afforded the only protection against the policies of an inflation-minded government.

While psychology is an important—yet superficial—speculative influence on the stock market, the mass reasoning out of which it evolves must always be detachedly appraised, for it is often productive of a popular delusion. The impermanence of the Coolidge-Hoover boom era was only too tragically demonstrated later in the worst depression on record.

On the opposite side, the belief that there was no end to adversity and that chaos began with the Banking Holidays of 1933 was just as thoroughly shattered by the series of New Deal measures, unorthodox to be sure, which reversed the deflationary trend. Still persisted in 1938, after a devastating stock market break and the most rapid business decline on record, the notion that inflation was an investment cure-all. All of these beliefs, viz., the unlimited prosperity of the 1920's, the interminable depression of 1929-32, and the inflation theory of 1933-38, have been responsible for a disastrous investment experience by many people.

To think that any popular belief in what the mysterious future holds is a quick solution of investment problems is quite certain to lead an investor into error. Without subscribing entirely to the law of action and reaction, it is nevertheless safe to assume that the pendulum will always swing from good times to bad, regardless of artificial measures.

Adherence to the view that equities and commodities are protection against prolonged inflation excludes both the classic examples of Germany and France and ignores the differences between American conditions and those abroad. The huge productive capacity of the United States, many industries of which could—if output were geared to the limit—within a few months inundate the market for goods, is the most marked differentiation. Secondly, there is the item of our huge natural resources. Thirdly, there is the tax factor, already so well developed as an inflation restraint. Finally, investigations will show that the *time elememt*, which is so frequently overlooked by constitutionally impatient Americans, is the biggest factor, since it took inflation 10 years in Germany and 14 years in France to run its course—if, indeed, it has run its course in France even yet.

Without delving into the actual results, which demonstrate that no one form of investment—real estate, commodities or stocks —was other than an inadequate "hedge", inflation is cited merely as the latest example of the skepticism with which the popular reasoning of any era must be regarded. After five years of inflation talk the *Dow-Jones* index of commodity futures (as of June 1, 1938) was not far from the lowest level for the $4\frac{1}{2}$-year period for which the computation has been made.

In the long run the so-called fundamentals have, in orthodox and unorthodox periods of finance, ultimately determined the major trend of the stock market. To the humorist, the "fundamentals" are the favorite Wall Street cliché. Yet these are the factors that must be constantly studied by investors and which, when properly understood, can make the financial columns as interesting to the well-versed reader as the sports or political pages.

The most driving and potent fundamental is earning power. It is the factor that the market is constantly endeavoring to appraise. If earnings are in the ascendancy, stocks are bound to rise. If a persistent decline in earnings is in force, then stocks are bound to fall.

Money and credit conditions constitute another but less important fundamental. All things being equal, easy money naturally makes cash unattractive and equities more desirable. But, it must be pointed out, before passing on to the later discussions of bull and bear markets, that major advances have occurred in a period of swollen credits and high money rates— as in the late '20s—and that major declines have set in—as in 1937—with abnormal money ease.

Politics, diplomacy, the spirit of enterprise and similar

additional considerations enter into the realm of fundamentals. These, however, are distinctly subsidiary. Boiled down, money and earnings are the imperishable influences on the course of the stock market. At the risk of repetition, *earning power* is dominant and warrants engrossing attention at all times.

CHAPTER THREE

Risk in All Business
Importance of Commodity Prices—"They" Can't
Move Stock Market—Tape Tells the Story

L EGITIMACY and inevitability of speculation, an appreciation of which must make for a realistic attitude toward so-
called investments, can be best comprehended by an understanding of business. Though "business risk" is a hackneyed expression, it seems frequently to be overlooked by purchasers of
stocks. Yet in all business there is risk, or, frankly, speculation.

When a business undertakes a contract it assumes many
hazards. If it is a raw material producer, it has to grow, mine
or extract the product and, in so doing, assume the speculative
risks of variable weather, labor, transportation conditions, and
the like. If it is a manufacturer, it must buy raw material,
fabricate that into goods, sell the goods in competition and collect
the bill before its job is done. If a merchant, it must buy in
advance and expose itself to the hazards of a fall in price or demand. Not until business closes the books at the end of the year
can it know exactly where it stands.

And what most determines business profits or losses at the
end of a year is the status of the inventory account. If a cotton
manufacturer buys his cotton too high, if a brass manufacturer
stocks up on high-priced copper, if a tire manufacturer mis-
judges the crude rubber market, then all the manufacturing
efficiency in the world and all of the most brilliant sales efforts in
the world will go by the boards. Red ink will be the lot of the businessman who woefully miscalculates the trend of inventory values.

The big Chicago packers represent the classic example of
how it is possible to make a lot of money in a rising market and

hand it back the next year in a period of declining prices. They operate on an exceedingly thin profit margin, and a decline in meat prices can play havoc on a turnover which, in the case of Swift & Co., for instance, ranges between $900,0C0,000 and $1,000,000,000 a year in good times.

As both manufacturer and merchant are constantly speculating on the trend of commodity values, the right guess is oftentimes the sole explanation of success. Saving of a cent a pound over competitors in the price of raw materials can outweigh oftentimes all the advantages of the most advanced manufacturing equipment. What is more, the year-end price of materials may be altogether out of line with values prevailing at the height of a selling season, so that a "pretty" inventory position during the year may turn out a colossal error when the final accounting is made.

If business were simply the conversion of raw materials into finished products to be sold at a standardized processing fee, then speculation would quickly be erased from the equation. Equities, which represent the ownership of business, would then lose their speculative mystery since their value could readily be determined by a growth or decline of sales.

Notorious is the textile industry for its varying fortunes. One has only to contrast the excellent profits of the first half of 1937 with the depressing losses for the full year. No better example of the speculative character of the textile business, which differs from general business only in the violence of its ups and downs, can be found than the experience of American Woolen Co. In early January, 1937, the management decided on a policy of extreme caution with respect to inventories. Raw wool holdings, which reached their peak almost at the beginning of the year at around 50,000,000 pounds, were steadily whittled down during the first half year. While American Woolen was rolling up profits of $3,400,000, its wool supplies were more than cut in two, to 20,000,000 pounds.

This policy was pursued until at the year-end the total was actually close to 3,000,000 pounds, the smallest aggregate on record. But in the meantime, by virtue of general price-cutting, a slump in sales and a sharp decline in wool values, the company had lost the $3,400,000 net of the first six months and $1,800,000 to boot. The shrewdest raw-material buying policies were vitiated by a sudden, engulfing depression.

Curiously enough, in this instance, the wool trade—not the company—was quick to place the blame on the comparatively new wool tops futures exchange. Like so many in the stock market who refuse to believe that a sudden rise or fall in prices betokens a drastic change for the better or worse in business some months hence, wool brokers were inclined to feel that the decline in wool futures had brought about the later decline in spot wool quotations.

Something of the same attitude prevailed in the terrific deflation of raw sugar between 1920 and 1921. Then the young Sugar Exchange (formed in 1914 as part of the New York Coffee and Sugar Exchange), where speculation for the decline was in full force before the crash in sugar from 22$\frac{1}{2}$ cents to less than two cents, was the alleged culprit. Now, however, the sugar futures market is actively and constantly used for hedging by sugar interests, and has come to be accepted as an integral part of the machinery of the sugar industry.

Speculation is constantly evolving, regardless of national measures to frustrate it, and the growth of the commodity exchanges, if properly regulated, may some day be regarded as a boon to the "ultimate consumer." Flour manufacturers confess that the wheat milling industry, which is so essential a part of the production of the staff of life, would undergo a revolution if the Chicago Wheat Pit were to be abolished. Who, say the biggest flour millers, would accept large contracts if they were unable to hedge actual raw material purchases, and whence would come the enormous amount of capital required to carry needed supplies of wheat? In financing the most staple article of diet, then, speculation serves a very useful function to the community.

In just the same manner, speculation, when not carried to excess, is of equal service in the stock market. The patient, courageous buyer of stocks when dire depression prevails provides a market many times for harassed businessmen, and then, through the willingness to accept a fair profit, reprovides stock for the businessmen buyers when the turn for the better is thoroughly apparent.

The short seller helps to check a boom and provides buying support when the business reverses which he visualized have materialized. While SEC studies show short selling accelerates a decline, nevertheless short covering at the bottom and the intrepid selling at the top correspond to the governor of a steam engine in helping to prevent the exercise of too great speculative pressure in either direction.

Wall Street sets the speculative tempo of the world. Time was when London was the dominant market. But now, in the maelstrom of disorganized or rapidly changing financial and business conditions abroad, America is the favorite investment center. Despite the SEC rules and restrictions, heavy arbitraging in international issues still takes place between New York and other centers. In International Nickel, for instance, New York is the balancing force through four-way arbitraging in the London, Montreal and Toronto markets. To the internationally-minded bankers of England, France, Switzerland and Holland the speculative pulse of the United States carries the most weight in diagnosing the future.

In "the good old days" a 7% turnover in a popular stock in a fortnight would have been commonplace. Gone for a long time, if not forever, are such days. At the same time, try as the SEC may to mitigate rapid price fluctuations, it will be helpless to prevent a broad movement of prices so long as the flux of business inherent to private management endures.

Granting the unquenchable nature of speculation, it is necessary to recognize that there are no mysterious "they" who move the stock market about at will. Even in the unbridled markets of 30 years ago as powerful a capitalist as H. H. Rogers, who conducted many a speculation in Amalgamated Copper, the predecessor of Anaconda, used ruefully to admit that he never knew for certain how the stock would open or close on any given day. Individuals and groups, like governments with commodities, have attempted to peg or permanently to elevate the price of stocks only to fail if fundamental conditions were inimical.

The idea that a group of "insiders" or dominant directors and officers of any company are so blessed with advance information, superior foresight and speculative daring as to be able at will to conduct a profitable operation in the stock is equally inaccurate. If the bank security company fiascoes of 1929-32 were not enough to shatter that naïve belief, the history of American International Corp., now a quiet and relatively little investment trust, may be recalled.

Organized in 1915 to do an international business and to foster a fast growing foreign trade, abnormally stimulated by war, and with a directorate which read like a Blue Book of finance and industry, AIC excited speculative imagination beyond credulity. On its board were most of the top "economic royalists" of that day. The stock zoomed to a huge premium on the capital which was provided in comfortable instalments, but it fell ignominiously in the commodity crash of 1920-21. Ultimately its glamorous-sounding foreign ventures had to be liquidated and the proceeds invested in conventional American equities.

Of course, nowadays the public has the benefit—if such it may be termed—of full publicity concerning the stock market buying and selling of all officers and directors, and of persons owning over 10% of the capitalizations of their companies. While the figures furnished by the SEC are necessarily a month or so late, the information is usually fresher than the vital earnings figures which customarily appear no oftener than quarterly. As to the value of knowing what insiders are doing, consider the past record. Some concentrated selling of a few stocks took place in the summer of 1937, but not on a large scale, since in the two months' period of rising prices, June 14-August 14, there were only eight sessions when trading exceeded 1,000,000 shares. Nothing occurred to indicate inside knowledge of the depression that was then in the actual making. To follow the transactions of insiders, which may simply revolve around the individual problem of income taxes, is no safe formula for the market place.

And the "insiders" apparently possessed no better market "smell" or prescience in the years gone by. The famous market manipulator of the early present century, James R. Keene, the man who "floated" the then unseasoned United States Steel common, maintained that hitting the market right three times out of five was enough to ensure a fortune. Reminded of that remark in the war boom, one of the most studious and best known Morgan partners exclaimed, "Even that margin of accuracy is impossible."

Just to show how Homer may nod, there is the following story vouched for by the individual who handled the trades. A prominent broker received directly from a senior partner of a famous banking house in the big spring rally of 1930, which followed the sensational break of October, 1929, an order for the purchase of 10,000 shares of Steel common "at market", then above 180. With questionable ethics, but commendable zeal and solicitude, he hastened to convey the information with appropriate plea for its confidential treatment to one of the famous bears of that period. The answer was characteristically swift: "First class. Sell me 10,000 shares short." As most people can recall, the trained speculator was right and the banker wrong, the sequel being a decline in United States Steel in 1932 into the lower 20's.

Of course, speculators are not 100% right in aiming for and assisting in establishing all price levels. American Telephone was depressed in 1932 below 70 and yet the $9 dividend, then rumored to be gravely jeopardized, has thus far remained inviolate. Going back to an earlier date, there was Studebaker which in the 1919-21 bear market, paying $7, went under 40. Instead of passing or lowering the $7 dividend rate, the company in the next two years went into the heyday of its prosperity and the stock rose by over $100 a share. But these examples are the exceptions rather than the rule, for market anomalies of unjustifiably high or small yields seldom persist.

"The tape tells the story" is the dictum accepted by those most versed in stock market lore. And, since the market cannot be made or unmade by "60 families" or by any individual or group, it is an arena in which the rewards are great for the exercise of proper judgment. Present-day rules of speculation are as fair as zealous legislation and progressive practices can possibly make them. That the term "lamb" has virtually disappeared from the lexicon of the day is the strongest bit of evidence of the safeguards afforded the public and of how much faith, in studying what appear at first as market vagaries, investors may place in the adage that "knowledge is power."

The initial philosophy with which the amateur or layman should face investment, or, in reality, speculative problems, is to look forward. There is no more sense in crying over spilt milk with respect to errors of judgment in Wall Street than there is in any other human experience. Stocks ultimately prove to have been cheapest when potential buying power was lowest, so, if bargains are missed, it is more often than not because of a general impairment of buying power shared by thousands. Speculation is always looking forward and is never concerned with the past. For proper poise every individual interested in the quotations on the New York Stock Exchange must always maintain a forward-looking attitude—must always try to visualize conditions some months hence.

For all the striving of the New Deal and the SEC, the stock market will never stand still. It is always moving in one direction or another. Movement in a restricted area seldom lasts for long. Sometimes, of course, the movement out of a stalemate may prove misleading, i. e., a reaction in a bull market or a rally in an incomplete bear market. Stagnation spells death, and a stable market would spell death to business, as we know it today, or would mark the end of its growth.

More helpful than to indulge in the instinctive yearning of mankind for economic stability is to grant at the outset that nothing stands still—least of all the stock market. Through the impact of the judgments of thousands of security owners it reflects business and political and financial developments the world over.   Consequently, the knowledge of paramount importance is the fundamental character of the stock market, bull or bear.   To invest money simply because cash is available is the worst mistake that can be made.   Just a moderate shrinkage in principal resulting from investing at an inopportune time can wipe out the dividends of several years.   Therefore, the most important phase of speculation is an understanding of the main trend.

CHAPTER FOUR

The Main Trend

Security Portfolios Are Inventories—Market Always "Bull" or "Bear"—Business Activity Must Be Watched

IF every owner of securities could once and for all realize that stocks are nothing more or less than fluctuating inventories, he would be entering the perplexing field of speculation with a hard-boiled, realistic point of view. The great bulk of investors, however, constitutionally come to regard stockholdings as permanent and as fixed a possession as the ownership of a home.

Bankers, however, who know from experience that both bonds and stocks can swing violently, by virtue of business conditions, earning power or interest rates, carry as a fixed inventory only cash. If securities were always rising, why should underwriting houses consummate new financing as quickly as possible? The cold fact is that cash will always bring 100 cents on the dollar, whereas stocks—because they reflect the fortunes of business—will always fluctuate. It is already a lively problem whether the SEC regulations have not made the stock market actually more volatile than it was in the unrestricted days.

Because of all this, knowledge of the underlying trend of the stock market is as vital to investors as judgment of raw material markets to manufacturers. A manufacturer never buys material simply because he has the cash. By the same token, an investor with funds ought not to rush into the market. The business man stocks up with goods from a conviction that a sustained rise in price is pending or because the demand for his finished products is such as to necessitate immediate buying. By the analogy of the operations of industry, the investor—who is really a speculator, whatever he thinks—should adopt the same standards of flexibility.

He should run strong in cash when deflation appears on the horizon or business clouds hang low. He should be heavily long of stocks only when the signs point clearly to an extended business rise or when security demand is such as to imply the release of powerful investment forces that may ultimately breed an era of speculation for the rise.

Paramount is the necessity of an independent conclusion concerning the underlying trend of the stock market. It is imperative for every individual to do his own thinking. In so doing he must be skeptical of political or industrial opinion, which, frequently verging on propaganda, may encourage the cheerful psychology that often proves the most superficial and ephemeral of all market influences. Bearish or bullish, he must resolutely resist that most seductive speculative evil, "wishful thinking"— the pitting of hope against fact.

Truest of speculative truisms is that the "stock market never stands still." The underlying trend may not portray itself for weeks or even for months, but it is a durable factor, its influence lasting for a year, and frequently for years. Once a fundamental trend is established, it maintains itself until new and more powerful forces operate to bring about a reversal of the movement.

A bull market is one in which successive rises top previous peaks until a clear-cut pattern of advance is established. It represents a collective preference for equities to cash, an insistent buying eagerness that is willing steadily to bid for stocks at advancing quotations. Conversely, a bear or declining market spells nothing more than a collective preference for cash and the willingness to secure the cash by offering stocks for sale at constantly lowering quotations. The phenomena of bull and bear markets will be treated in subsequent chapters.

Granting the premise that the stock market never stands still, but, in the recurrent periods of indecisive movement, is simply accumulating energy for a vigorous thrust upward or downward, it must be obvious that to buy stocks on a large scale —which is to say, for the average individual to be more or less fully invested—implies a definite belief in the existence of a bull market. Conversely, to assume a preponderantly cash position implies a conviction of a protracted downtrend of quotations. Failure to observe the logic of this simple conclusion, i. e., that the market is definitely in a bull or bear movement, is the cause of some of the most damaging of investment errors. Merely because the worst in business and finance seems to have been discounted or fully appraised is no sufficient reason to buy stocks after a steep decline. There must be assurance that conditions may not become worse, or, in other words, that a bear market has run its course.

On the other hand, because a substantial rise has occurred is no reason to sell stocks, especially since bull markets consume a much longer period than do bear markets. Like all build-ings, speculative edifices are torn down faster than they are erected. Premature selling in a bull market can be just as damaging in the curtailment of potential profit as the hasty buying of stocks before the completion of all the liquidating phases of a bear market.

Once an opinion is formed concerning the real character of the stock market (it can be only "bull" or "bear") an investor should follow the hoary axiom of "never buck the trend." Professionals have another phrasing of the same advice—"never quarrel with the tape." The folly of assuming investment positions that are at variance with the main trend has been demonstrated over and over again, and it is just as painful in its effect on security portfolios as guessing commodity markets is to business profits.

Just here the corrective philosophy that "the stock market can do anything" must necessarily be interpolated. Prices can rise temporarily in the face of the worst news and can fall despite the most encouraging developments.

As an illustration of the sometimes inexplicable perversity of the stock market, recall the occasion in 1915 during the early part of the World War when the first pages of all the newspapers were literally covered with sensational headlines of the destruction of the British fleet in the Dardanelles. On that day the stock market had a big rise, to the amazement of almost everybody. But the situation evidently was that the market required no liquidation. Enormous war orders were pouring in, and, consequently, no attention was paid to the naval reverse that constituted the big news of the day.

Stressing the necessity of arriving at an opinion on the main trend places emphasis on the conservation or the enhancement of principal. Putting capital to work at somewhere near the most attractive buying level in a bull market will produce far more profit to the investor than dividends from an inopportunely timed investment.

Too often investors refuse to sell because income is thereby temporarily relinquished. Yet it ought to be apparent that the loss of several points in principal will, in most cases, wipe out at least the full dividend return for a year. People who were buying Chrysler around 135 in the summer of 1937, when its brilliant record of dividend liberality was attracting most attention, would in a little over a year have suffered a 100 point loss, or a 75% shrinkage in principal with a temporary cessation of dividend payments to boot. Stocks must never be bought for "keeps".

A field where correct judgment can bring enormous returns can hardly be an exact science. Too many factors, visible and invisible, enter into the shaping of a speculative current. Mistakes are always possible and errors will always be made in gauging the character of the stock market. Still it is possible to gain a working knowledge of the factors that bring about the recurrent market upheavals that, it is now demonstrated, can take place even in a quasi-managed economy.

Of all the fundamental, lasting influences on the stock market the most powerful, by all odds, is the aggregate earning power of business. Real estate, farms, mines, businesses of every description are bought on some basis that capitalizes profits—present and prospective. In its entirety the stock market, in the last analysis, is always endeavoring to capitalize the near-term and the much more illusory long-term trend of earnings. Not the past results, but the trend of earnings is what influences stock prices.

How much importance successful speculators attach to earnings may be judged by the point of view of Bernard M. Baruch. The man who made a fortune in Wall Street, and kept it, to become an important adviser of national Administrations ever since the days of Woodrow Wilson, was once interviewed by a cub financial reporter young enough to stand in no awe of the Baruch name. The interview occurred in the early months of 1930 when the market was enjoying a sensational rebound from the October, 1929, panic. As the meeting took place around four o'clock, the ambitious journalist carried in his hands a copy of his evening paper.

Baruch, reaching for the paper, spread it out on a desk and glanced down at the column of stock market gossip. It contained several references to brokers who had bought 20,000 shares and 10,000 shares of Radio and similar favorites of that bygone era. Pounding on the desk, Baruch exclaimed "What good are all these names and what do they mean? Why don't you tell what the stocks are earning? That's all that matters!" Then, pointing to certain railroad carloading figures, he added, "Why, even these railroad statistics tell something," and proceeded to demonstrate what contraction in traffic probably meant in dollars and cents to the carriers.

Although a great many corporations publish quarterly earnings with a fair degree of promptitude, it is not always possible for the layman far removed from the byways of the financial district to learn exactly what is taking place in the income account of companies in which he may be most interested. Especially in the transition from good times to bad, or vice versa, may the news of the significant turn be hard to gather, for frequently business executives themselves are swept off their feet by the rapidity of a collapse or an improvement in trade.

Hence the first approach to the broad scope of earning power must be the study of the trend of business activity. If the steam in the business boiler is steadily rising, prosperity is probably in the making or still prevails. If the gauge is falling, then recession or depression may be on its way. In either event, one should be watching.

In following the business trend the student of the market may watch the fluctuations in output and consumption of certain

TRENDS OF STOCKS AND BUSINESS COMPARED

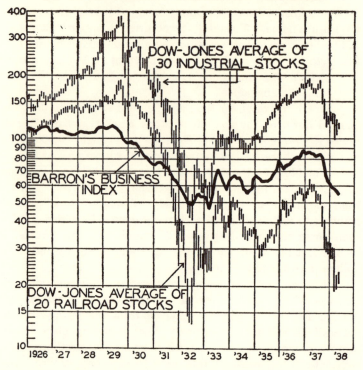

basic commodities such as steel, cotton, automobiles, etc. He must also watch the movement of certain simple, accepted indicators of business activity such as steel operations, electric power consumption, and revenue freight carloadings. But there are several easily accessible indexes of the trend of general business which combine all these indicators and give a broad view of what is going on in industry and trade in general. These indexes do not, of course, fluctuate so sensitively as indicators of particular lines, but they are more reliable barometers of the major trend.

Barron's compiles such an index of production and trade. This index is a measure of the physical volume of manufacturing and mining output, electric power production, freight carloadings and building. It is computed on both a monthly and a weekly basis.

The close relation between business activity and major stock price movements is clearly revealed by this chart. Over the years the two have moved along parallel lines over four fifths of the time. In 1929 *Barron's* Business Index reached its high point of 115.1 in June, while the *Dow-Jones* industrial share average did not reach its climax until September. So also, prior to the severe depression of 1937-1938, business hit its high ahead of the stock market.

As gauged by the monthly index, business activity had climbed to 88.8% of normal in December, 1936. From this high point it dropped off a little during the spring and summer of 1937, but it was still as high as 85.4% in August. From this level, however, it experienced the most rapid drop since 1893. Industrial stock prices were behind in making their high, the average climbing to a recovery peak of 194.40 on March 10, 1937, from which it declined. By Aug. 14, 1937, the *Dow-Jones* industrial share average had again reached 190.02, from which point it dropped to a low of 113.64 by November 24. Failure of *Barron's* Business Index after eight months to better its earlier high was a healthy warning in 1937 of possible breakers ahead for the stock market.

Industrial production may be divided into two main types, broadly speaking, that of durable or producers' goods and consumers' goods. In studying business trends, appreciation of the significance of these two groups is important.

From a forecasting or barometric point of view, changes in the demand for durable goods are of the greater significance, since it is the purchase, and, therefore, production of these that indicate the outlook for business in general and reflect the sentiment and judgment of business leaders. These purchases can be deferred when times are bad and the outlook clouded, whereas consumers' goods, to a certain degree, are in steady demand in good or bad times. Consumers' goods output, therefore, fluctuates less widely and is a less sensitive index, although it necessarily reflects to some degree public purchasing power. On the other hand, activity of the heavy or durable goods industries is extremely sensitive to current business conditions and to the business outlook.

Another important indicator of business conditions and prospects, and one which has been slow to show progress in the recent recovery movement from the 1932-33 depression low, is the volume of capital expenditures. These usually involve issuance of new securities by corporations to raise money for plant improvements, machinery, equipment and extension of facilities. It is only when some confidence is felt in what the future holds that such responsibilities are undertaken. That is why so much is heard in depressions of "business must take hold."

CHAPTER FIVE

Buy "Earnings", not "Dividends"

Commodities as a Barometer—Importance of the
Bond Market—Dividends Carry Little Speculative
Weight

THERE is no easy "success" formula for perfection in security
operations, and business activity alone is not an accurate
index of actual earning power. Recall for instance, the "profitless
prosperity" of a decade ago. At that time certain industries,
notably textiles, were operating at a high rate but, because of
the slim margin of profit, were making little or no money. Again,
there is the more recent and familiar example of the utilities,
which found a terrific expansion of electricity production largely
nullified by stringently high taxes or by a low level of rates forced
by governmentally financed competition. Just a thorough-
going reading of the daily newspapers will serve to bring into
focus factors that may modify the significance of a cold, statistical record of business activity.

Second in importance in forecasting the probable general
course of industrial earning power is the trend of commodity
prices. There are several good commodity price indexes based
on quotations of a large number of representative commodities,
the fluctuations of which are of real import to American industry.
Best known of this type of index is the Bureau of Labor Statistics
index of wholesale commodity prices which is compiled from
over 800 quotations. Plainly, a rise in commodity prices spells
an appreciation of business inventories, tends to stimulate buying and thus to improve both the margin of profit and the volume
of sales—which are the elementary factors in the determination
of earnings.

A persistent rise in commodities almost invariably heralds

the quickening of buying and the expansion of activity, provided the development does not occur after an extended period of rising prices or active business operations. Just as definitely ominous is the significance of a steady decline in commodity prices in harbingering deflation, which is the wrecker of earning power.

While the spot commodity price index is most valuable, because it denotes just what business, in dealing with the tangible realities of supply and demand, is willing to pay, the index of commodity futures prices is helpful in the light it throws on speculative or forward operations. A violent rise or fall in commodity futures prices tells what the expectations are for several months ahead. A brisk, sustained move in the commodity futures market is usually a precursor of a similar movement in

CHART 1

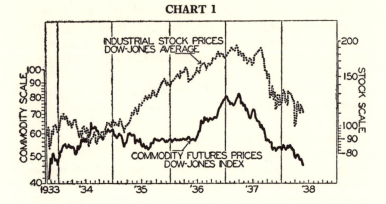

spot prices, and contrariwise. Best of commodity futures indexes is the *Dow-Jones* index which includes prices of commodities in an adequate number of active raw material markets, viz: cocoa, coffee, corn, cotton, hides, rubber, oats, rye, silk, sugar and wheat.

Refinement of the study of commodity prices in their bearing on business earning power and thus, in turn, on the stock market, may be had by recourse to a sensitive spot commodity price index. *Barron's* index of sensitive spot prices is based on quotations of the following 13 commodities: Burlap, cotton print cloths, cottonseed oil, hides, lard, rubber, shellac, silk, steel scrap, tallow, wheat, wool and zinc.

Most valued single barometric item is steel scrap, the price of which is available in any metropolitan newspaper. A sudden drop in steel scrap is usually the forerunner of a let-down in steel operations. Similarly, the failure of steel scrap to advance after a precipitous drop ordinarily betokens an extended depression. An upturn usually forecasts higher steel operations.

Almost as important as steel scrap to business and security market calculations is the price of copper. It is the raw material of the electric age in which we live. It is also a vital war material and demand for munitions exercises a strong effect on its price. Because copper enters into the manufacturing processes of such major industries as automobiles and electrical equipment, etc., its price trend always carries great weight in business planning.

Third factor to be followed faithfully in analyzing the main stock market trend is the movement of the bond average. It is portrayed in the *Dow-Jones* average of 40 bonds published daily. It comprises 10 high-grade rail, 10 second-grade rail, 10 public utility and 10 industrial bonds. Marked strength or weakness in any of the four departments should be cause for concern as possibly likely to initiate a trend in the general average. Rising or falling bond yields, when contrasted with stock yields, serve to show the relative attractiveness of outright investment media against business-risk equities.

The three factors enumerated, (1) business activity, (2) commodity prices and (3) the bond market, all to be followed through conventional indexes registering rise or fall, portray, respectively, the strength of business activity, the tempo of speculation in business and the underlying attitude of investment capital—whether confident or defeatist. The first two bear on the earning power that is the crux of the speculative problem and will be dealt with in more detail later, while the last sets the price on what is naturally regarded as safer capital. Barring war, famine and acts of God, the trinity of factors enumerated is continuously operating on Stock Exchange quotations to make a bull or a bear market.

Inasmuch as restive speculation is always looking forward in the attempt to anticipate changing conditions, the records of current business activity and present earning power are insufficient for the formulation of a theory on the character of the main trend. That is, they delineate only the week-to-week happenings and cannot, except as a definite trend develops, infallibly forecast ahead.

An ideal business index for speculative guidance would be one that registered the volume of forward buying. Such a type of statistical record would portray with what rapidity the tide of business was flowing, as measured by manufacturing needs for actual sales requirements, and it would at the same time tell whether inventories were inadequate or excessive. If a comprehensive index of forward buying were obtainable, and this is not yet evolved because of the reluctance of individual businesses to disclose trade secrets, then the world at large could have prompt knowledge of the effect of sales volume on inventories, the fluctuations of which play so big a part in earning power.

Everything bearing on earning power should be seized and scrutinized by a wide-awake investor. It is the climb of earning power and the clear-cut projection of an upward profits curve that stimulate enthusiasm amongst business executives. It is what produces the "businessman buying" of stocks that is always the most convincing in a rising market. Undiluted business optimism based on tangible realities is as conducive to a healthy rise as word-of-mouth approval by the public is to the success of a new play.

With the number of listed stocks on the New York Stock Exchange running into four figures, a complete survey of business earning power is a task hardly worth the effort. In the first place, there are less than 100 major companies, the trends of which—because of their size and type of business—satisfactorily portray the national profits curve. Their figures reflect prosperity or depression in farming, mining, petroleum, automotive, steel and the major manufacturing and distributing activities.

A serious market student should, then, keep track of the earnings of the major industrials for which, in many instances, quarterly reports are available (shown in the *At a Glance* pages of *Barron's*). The railroads report monthly and their status can be easily followed. A good many utilities publish monthly figures that shed a clear light on their progress. Digesting these earnings reports takes time but it is the only way to tell which way the profits wind is blowing.

Too many people, who regard the financial columns as boring as the women's page, prefer to allow dividends to spell the measure of corporate prosperity. But it cannot be too strongly emphasized that dividends are of no value, in most cases, in determining market quotations. During the war Bethlehem Steel climbed over 500 points before distributing $1 of its huge gains. In fact, its executive head liquidated 10,000 shares before the rise began, on the theory that working capital and plant needs would for years necessitate plowing back of war profits into the business. His judgment, which was based on dividend rather than earnings prospects, was singularly inept. Again, General Motors, in the first phase of its amazing growth under Boston banking management, climbed to fancy prices before the Durant management regained control and released a fortune of earning power to stockholders.

From another angle, dividends of themselves prove quite misleading. When American Locomotive in 1925 increased the regular rate to $8 from $6 and at the same time ordered a $10 extra payable in four quarterly instalments, Wall Street jumped to the conclusion that the $2.50 extra dividend was a regular feature. The stock soared 40 points close to 145, but three years later, despite progress of an unparalleled bull market, it was selling around 87. What had happened was that the big locomotive-building company had simply lopped off the fat conserved from the war boom years earlier and the dividend largesse in no wise measured current or prospective earnings.

Under the undistributed-profits tax in force during 1936 and 1937, stock market conclusions based on dividend payments would also have gone sadly awry. Nearly every big company, and certainly every concern that had ample financial resources, naturally preferred to pay out the bulk of its earnings. Witness what happened: Chrysler, which paid $12 in 1936 and $10 in 1937, paid nothing in the first quarter of 1938, and only 50 cents in the second quarter (June 14); and Johns-Manville, which paid $4.75 in 1937, including a year-end extra of $1, suspended payments before spring rolled around.

Before the creation of the SEC there were those who, ignoring both earnings and dividends, thought the ticker tape told the entire story. Reams have been written in years gone by concerning the technique of tape reading, viz., how to detect "distribution" or "accumulation" and how to tell when a sharp move was at hand. Much of this theorizing was based on so-called "volume" indications. Even in the period of pools, untrammeled "insider" operations and manipulation, the phenomena of tape reading were frequently misleading. In any event, with the advent of the SEC and the attendant elimination of artificial buying or selling, and all of the other measures that have created tragically thin markets, tape reading is a lost art.

No consideration has thus far been given to money rates as a factor in shaping the main market trend because the experience of the writer has been that money rates are rarely a major influence. High money rates were no barrier to climbing stocks in 1907 and 1929; ludicrous money ease was no dam to the liquidation of 1937.

The bond market is a sufficient guide to the effect of money on the main body of stocks. Of collateral help is the contrast in the rate commanded by money and the yields from high-grade bonds and the choicest, seasoned stocks. All things being equal, which means business being good and earning power buoyant, a favorable disparity in yield from money rates and the yields from seasoned stocks is bound, of course, in due time to make securities in demand.   Stocks necessarily become more valuable than cash.

A factor of no fundamental worth, but one which has to be reckoned with on many occasions, is speculative psychology. Unreasoned, emotional mass attitude toward stocks can wield a great deal of influence on prices. "Sentiment" is superficial and, except occasionally for periods like the '20s, seldom lasting. It is most deceptive at the top of a bull swing, when everyone you meet is cheerful, and at the bottom of a bear swing, when every-

CHART II

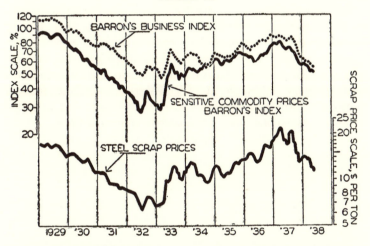

Barron's Business Index, as charted, is adjusted for long-term trend. *Barron's* Sensitive Spot Commodity Price index is relative to 1926. The steel scrap price curve is based on the *Iron Age* average of quotations at Pittsburgh, Philadelphia and Chicago.

one encountered is gloomy.   The astute investor must guard against the infection of speculative psychology.

In the self-discipline that comes from factual study of the market and careful reasoning processes, the cultivation of patience—the cardinal virtue in investment as well as in living— may become easier.   One of the shrewdest broker-bankers, who died worth $50,000,000, once said "There are hundreds of men in Wall Street with sound judgment but only one in a thousand with the requisite patience." What he meant was that every major move should be played to the limit, and, in so speaking, he merely re-emphasized the need of knowledge concerning the main market trend.

Just to show what veteran brokers think of the average speculator, a partner of a big New York commission house once said, after a typical, devastating decline, "There must be an awful lot of money made in business or otherwise where would the money that our clients lose so blithely come from?" A prominent New England industrialist of 20 years ago who, because of stubbornness, lost millions in New Haven railroad, once admitted to the writer, "I don't suppose I've ever made any money to speak of outside of my own business." Random stories of this description illustrate the losses that come even to successful business men from ignorance of fundamental, elementary stock market factors. What few people recognize is that speculators, not so-called investors, make and always will make the market trend.

CHAPTER SIX

Charts as Weather Vanes

Charts Helpful at Top and Bottom—The Stock
Market is Always Saying Something

SOMEWHAT akin to the tape readers are the chart analysts.
By plotting a line showing the day-to-day trend, or even
the hour-to-hour trend, of quotations and coupling it with lines
of volume of trading, they have a common belief that therefrom
appears the clue to the near-term movement of the stock market.
The underlying theory is, of course, that in the general market
and individual stocks the fluctuations are always plotting out
a line which, when reduced to graphic form, shows the direction
in which a forthcoming movement of importance will take place.
There is a good deal to be said for chart reading in its broadest
aspect, showing at a glance to the layman—who usually lacks
the time or facilities to retain a vivid impression of price forma-
tions—whither the market may be drifting or sailing.

Fundamentally, however, a chart is no more or less than a
weather vane. It may at a given moment be pointing, for
instance, southwesterly, which would betoken calm weather; yet
it can swing suddenly in the opposite direction, which would spell
stormy weather. And it is the veering of direction that causes
devastation among investors.

No formula can be derived from chart reading that will
insure speculative accuracy any more than a system can be devised for choosing winners of horse-races from past performance.
The forces at work in the determination of a major price movement are too deep-seated to be reflected in a simple instrument
that merely records fluctuations and for that reason confident
reliance can never be placed upon chart reading.

Charts are obviously of value in registering the progress and force of an advance or decline. If in a bull market a previous high point is emphatically penetrated on a substantial volume of trading, the inference plainly is that the vigor of speculative fermentation is increasing and that a new phase of the rise is at hand. Conversely, if a previous low for the market is broken on active trading, then the inference is equally strong that the pressure of liquidation has increased to a degree that probably spells another chapter in the downward movement. If interpreted in the fashion of a clinical thermometer, charts are capable of showing whether the speculative fever is rising or falling.

In helping to clarify the confusion of thought which attends the culmination of a bull market or the termination of a bear market charts probably serve their greatest purpose. Obviously, the most vital decision that must be made in stockmarket operations and, therefore, the most difficult, is the diagnosis of the approaching end of a big upward swing or of the symptoms that herald the death of a liquidating movement. In the swirl of good news and excitement that accompanies the climax of a bull market and in the defeatist gloom and depressingly small dealings that ordinarily occur at the bottom of the bear market, it is hard for the most astute, realistic and unemotional investor to keep his head.

Opinions differ as to which is the more difficult decision, viz., to call the top of a bull market or the bottom of a bear market. Lord Rothschild years ago said that he got rich by never attempting—and, impliedly, by never hoping—to get the very top or the very bottom. Modern-day speculators have racily summed the problem up in the aphorism "the middle slice of cake should be enough for anyone."

Nonetheless, to secure the utmost return from employment of capital—to strive for perfection—it is imperative to allow major market movements to run to somewhere near the point where a metamorphosis occurs. In a bull market the usual signs are excessive activity, especially in the most speculative issues, and periodic uprushes in individual stocks—all taking place while the market as a whole is making relatively little progress.   As able a student of the stock market as the veteran editor of *The Wall Street Journal*, the late W. P. Hamilton, author of *The Stock Market Barometer*, always maintained that the dénouement of a bull market was usually portrayed rather clearly.

On the other hand, it has always seemed to the writer that the establishment of a bottom of a bear market was easier to locate. The phenomena are universal discouragement in financial and business circles and widespread unemployment throughout the country—all accompanied by a prolonged period of agonizing dullness during which the market, having discounted the worst, refuses to sink.

Now the conventional charts, embracing both prices and volume of transactions, clearly portray the excitement that has always in the past characterized the end of a cycle of enthusiasm. And especially are the charts of the general market serviceable when contrasted with what may be deceptive movements and dealings in individual issues.   The tracing of a bottom is ordinarily clearly portrayed by charts.

Always it must be borne in mind that the stock market is "saying something."   To the speculatively learned it should always have a message.   Oftentimes the message may be cryptic or may take time to decipher, but it is there just the same.   In the panic of October, 1937, there were actually people who maintained that, because earnings at that moment were so good, the collapse in prices could be ignored.

To that thesis, i. e., that a stock market movement could be disregarded, the comment of a hardboiled industrialist—whose responsibility it is to sell $400,000,000 of merchandise annually to the American people—may be of interest.   At that time he said, "No one can tell me that a $15,000,000,000 shrinkage in security market values can be ignored."   And, of course, the sequel was the most rapid decline in business activity on record.

Then there are the self-satisfied and the bewildered, to whom ignorance will always be bliss, who are amused or annoyed by a sudden jump or dip in the stock market on some apparently trivial development.   Theirs is the reasoning that could see in the difficulties surrounding the former king of England in marrying an American divorcee merely a frustrated romance instead of a parliamentary crisis. To be sure, Wall Street, which always feels it incumbent to offer some explanation or other of every stock market development, may unduly stress the trivial, yet banking and brokerage near-sightedness should not obscure the fact that the market is always actually moving in one direction or another, for a reason.

"The news favors the trend" is another axiom. Boiled down, it means that business, financial or political developments usually synchronize with the main trend of the market. If a market is rising, the presumption is that earnings are mounting, and, consequently, the publication of a favorable report stimulates new buying. Conversely, a slump in profits or a reduction in dividends is the logical concomitant of declining prices.

Too often politics is made the culprit for changes for the better or worse. Years ago, when the industrial and financial East was in the saddle in Washington, it used plaintively to be thought that bull markets could flourish only under a Republican Administration. The "full dinner-pail" slogan of the McKinley era helped for years to convince employers and wage earners, as well, that factory chimneys belched smoke only when the GOP was in charge of the National Government.

However, a brilliant bull movement took place during the first Wilson Administration. Although it was attributable to war prosperity, the point is that politics could not prevent it. And there was also the post-bellum boom of the second Wilson Administration.

Under the return to Republicanism with President Harding occurred the slump of 1920-21. Then came the most extended bull market on record during the presidential terms of Calvin Coolidge. The credit inflation of the foolish 1920's, it may be noted in passing, was made possible by the instrument of the Federal Reserve System fashioned under the Wilson Administration.

In more recent years there is the similar spectacle of the complete collapse of business and markets under Herbert Hoover, the abortive recovery and then the prolonged rise in the first Administration of Franklin D. Roosevelt. Finally came the inevitable aftermath of a sickening bear market in spite of the New Deal and all of its inflationary powers.

Therefore, it can be taken for granted by now that American business men are practical enough to want to adjust themselves as best they may to any kind of Administration and to any type of politics it may provide. The adjustment may be difficult or easy, the problems old or new, but adjustment is sure to be made. So long as private enterprise prevails, business, if only in obedience to the law of self-preservation, will strive to profit. Regardless of politics, rising or falling earning power will always be the strongest driving power in the stock market.

According to the Old Testament "There is no new thing under the sun." The New Deal is admittedly fantastic to any student of economics or any worshipper of the orthodox, yet under the Wilson Administration there was a "New Freedom" which, on a good many occasions, seemed just as baleful.

It is possible to draw a parallel of present-day conditions under Franklin D. Roosevelt with those of 30 years ago under Theodore Roosevelt. There were the same attacks on wealth, the same hostility to Wall Street, apprehension over the future of railroads, acute business depression and unemployment, loss of profits everywhere and a severe shrinkage of security values.

"Malefactors of great wealth," coined by TR, is not vastly different from the "economic royalists" of FDR. In due course came a shift in the political winds with the election of Secretary of War Taft and a new boom was on.

It might be deduced from paralleling the events of now and those of 30 years ago that politics brought about the panics of 1907 and 1937. It would be easy to jump to that conclusion. Yet one has only to read Alexander Dana Noyes's classic "*Forty Years of American Finance*" to appreciate the unbridled speculation and strain on credit that produced the money panic of 1907. Months earlier, as noted a banker as Jacob H. Schiff had warned of the inevitable disaster. And any fair-minded analyst of today will ascribe as the fundamental cause of the collapse of 1937 the dangerous expansion of inventories brought about by business programs based on a prospective inflation of labor and materials. While politics played its part on both occasions, 1907 and 1937, the stock market in neither year would have collapsed had it not been for unhealthy underlying business practices.

Another recognition of the inevitability of change may be found in the biblical conception of seven lean years and seven fat years. From that notion has evolved a speculative formula. Based on the record from 1893 to 1924, it called for a major market collapse every seven years and a minor collapse every subsequent three years. The years 1893, 1900, 1907, 1914 and 1921 were those of major buying points; 1896, 1903, 1910, 1917 and 1924 minor buying periods. The schedule went off the tracks in 1924 and 1931. However, the periodicity of the recurrence of good times and bad is too elementary to require elaboration in its bearing on a study of major stockmarket trends.

CHAPTER SEVEN

Bull Markets—The Best Buys

Bull Markets Offer Biggest Opportunities—Always
Some Outstanding Group—How to Select the
Leaders

TOO often investors buy long before a decline is ended, merely because prices have fallen so far, or sell too early because prices have risen so rapidly. It is never the level of prices *but the direction of the movement* that should count. Once "in" an investor should stay put and, though keenly following news affecting the market, should not be jumping in and out at the whim of emotional thinking. In business, as with the ocean, the tide will always continue to flow in and out. There is no good in looking backwards, for the Stock Exchange is always here tomorrow.

Since the American temperament is proverbially optimistic, speculation flourishes most actively in a bull market. It is common knowledge that the public at large never trades actively except for the rise, not only because short selling is unpopular and little understood but also because falling prices imply contraction of all forms of money-making activities including speculation.

Moreover, a bull market permits of the use of borrowed capital, the lifeblood of business growth and speculative activity. Fundamentally, it is impossible to utilize credit in sizable volume in a bear market, regardless of the new restrictions and high marginal requirements against short sales promulgated by the Securities and Exchange Commission. Banks cannot lend on short commitments as they can on purchases.

Bull markets, however, are no assured blessing to every security holder. In the rank inflation of the 1920's the abnormal rise in common stock valuations and the tremendous uplift in dividends, both cash and stock—all accompanied by the typical increase in living costs and extravagant living standards—put the bondholders (with a fixed income) at a decided disadvantage. Ordinarily, though, with a sane bull market goes a healthy appreciation in bond prices.

Since bull markets follow in the wake of bear markets, the conditions precedent to a dynamic advance are those brought about by the completion of liquidation. In other words, the first essential is ordinarily a "sold out" stock market, best denoted by a moderate or meager volume of stock brokerage loans. The test afforded by the aggregate of speculative borrowings is, however, by no means trustworthy of itself. The entire 1933-37 rise involved an increase to only $1,187,279,000 in the volume of stock brokerage loans, reported weekly by the Federal Reserve Board and monthly by the New York Stock Exchange, as against a 1929 peak of $8,549,384,000.

Of far greater necessity is the liquidated business status, since—whatever any one may think—it is business that makes the stock market, and not vice versa. When commodity prices have undergone a severe decline and leveled off, when inventories have been cut down to subnormal proportions, when business has undergone retrenchment, and when the public prefers—from necessity or choice—to save rather than to spend, then, truly, liquidation has run its course. Any change must be for the better and, because of what has gone before, the change, as it evolves, is likely to become marked.

Here, again, it is necessary to note exceptions to the rule. The unexpected bull market that followed the Armistice in 1918, for instance, took off from an industrial state in which inventories were high. The sequel to such an unorthodox bull market was the steep deflation of 1920-21 which played havoc with scores of companies and, for the first time, made "inventory control" a cardinal principle of corporate management. The exception noted with respect to the necessity of low brokerage loans and business inventories as precursors of a bull market should not minimize the importance of both items. By and large, a liquidated financial and business structure is obviously the soundest base upon which a healthy and enduring new structure of prosperity can be erected.

Sometimes when the stock market appears to have been liquidated, a frozen bond market may exist, as witness the situation in the fall of 1937 when the Bethlehem Steel Corp. bonds and Pure Oil Co. preferred issues landed almost in their entirety in the laps of the underwriters. A "sticky" bond market may easily be overlooked. It was back in the "rich men's panic" of 1903 that James J. Hill, sensing the gravity of overloaded underwriting syndicates, coined the expression "indigestible securities."

In the fruition of a bull market, along with liquidated security markets and business, a placid political atmosphere and a spirit of enterprise are helpful. Both were powerful forces in the 1920's under a Republican administration that had sharply lowered the high wartime income tax levies on business and individual incomes. Radical revision of the capital gains tax and virtual elimination of the undistributed-profits tax on May 27th, 1938, may, sometime hence, be regarded as of greater significance than the market indicated at the time the measure became law.

With all the various fundamentals existent to set a bull market in motion, there must be the prospect of a lessened value for cash. Expressed the other way, stocks must have a greater appeal than cash.

If the liquidation prior to the emergence of a bull market has been of an engulfing nature, including bonds as well as stocks, then the first sign of convalescence in the security markets is a persistent and extended rise in bonds. An improving bond market is telltale evidence of a return of investment confidence.

Once the bond market reflects the presence of an active demand that can be satisfied only at rising prices, then the return on bonds should be contrasted with the yield from the highest-grade common stocks. If the disparity is definitely in favor of stocks, then the inference is that an investment demand is in the making that is certain ultimately to spill over into stocks—usually preferred stocks first and common stocks later. Thus bonds show the way and stocks follow.

Sometimes blind faith is of more help than all the statistics in the world. The bank holidays of March, 1933, clearly represented the culmination of over three years of liquidation. Not even in the panic of 1907 had it been necessary to shut up the national banking system. Improvement had to follow so great a crisis or otherwise both the banking and business systems could not survive. But such buying opportunities occur only a few times in a lifetime. Few people get in on the ground floor because of the decimation of capital or because of fright, as in 1933.

Yet astute, professional speculators, quick to sense a trend, could see at the very beginning of the Roosevelt Administration which way the winds were likely to blow. The biggest American speculator of all time, vacationing in Florida during the bank holidays, told the writer, "Watch silver, cotton, wheat and New York Central—but silver first, last and all the time." As an idea of how big a plunger he was, his long position in 1930 was over 500,000 shares and, simply as a hedge, his short position totaled over 300,000 shares.

This individual was quick to read the handwriting on the wall. All that his market philosophy meant was that a soft money Administration, which in the Presidential campaign had refused to pledge itself to the maintenance of the gold standard, was certain to embark on a silver-buying program. In only a few weeks "something for silver" was a by-word in Washington and Wall Street, and silver stocks proved more sensational than gold in the early talk of inflation. Recommendation of cotton and wheat buying simply anticipated the already manifest solicitude for the farmer and the subsequently announced intention of the President to raise commodity prices at any cost. The least profitable of the four speculative suggestions, New York Central, foreshadowed the pledge to assist the railroads, an agreement that to time of this writing was never executed.

The actual arrival of a bull market is obviously attested by a rise in stock prices, with each surge upward surpassing the previous top. The most widely accepted barometer of the trend is the *Dow-Jones* industrial-share average, which comprises 30 representative issues, the movements of which afford an accurate picture of the main trend. There are averages composed of a much larger number of issues, but the greater the number the smaller the movement, and, consequently, the less easy to discern. Studies have proved that only a handful of issues move contrary to the trend reflected by the averages, which may consequently be accepted as a serviceable barometer.

While the early stages of a bull market, once the fundamentals for its genesis are established, is accompanied by an increase in the volume of trading and a persistent lift in the averages, there are usually outriding stocks that forge ahead of the main list. They are the pioneers of the movement into new territory. Sometimes such issues are merely a few of the standard speculative favorites that are first seized on by professionals in their traditional rôle of exploring the line of least resistance. Frequently, however, the celerity of the advance of individual stocks may betoken their sudden rise to stardom in the newly opened speculative drama. If two or more of the advance guard of a bull movement fall into a definite grouping, say steels, motors, utilities, chemicals, etc., then the significance may be even more marked, for the fashions change in the stock market just as they do with wearing apparel.

Thirty years ago railroad stocks were the most favored speculative vehicles. Then came the "war brides" and motor issues during the feverish war prosperity, and in the '20s—the utilities. Chain-store stocks, now in the discard, have had their day and chemicals, because of low labor costs and the record of the past 20 years, still enjoy an unusual rating. In every bull market there is invariably an outstanding group.

How to pick that group to produce better-than-average profits is another matter. Careful comparison of the trend of individual groups with the general market is obviously the first step. General psychology, to be gathered from the comment of brokerage houses and statistical advices, is an essential part of the manufacture of popularity. Above all, however, is the element of a background suddenly coming into focus.

For, though speculation never looks backward, a promising immediate past—susceptible of becoming a glowing future—is what attracts the shrewd, large-scale buyers. The utilities, for instance, had an impressive record prior to the 1924-29 boom which had simply been overlooked in the excitement of the war and after-war periods. The point was that "fat" in the shape of surplus earning power had been accumulating which was certain to be fried out in the shape of dividend largesses in the next period of business activity.

In fact, the first inkling that corporations were disposed to release the remainder of surplus earnings husbanded during the warj boom came with the 25-cent extra in late 1923 of the United States Steel Corp. It proved to be the precursor of a long period of higher dividends. In the absence of unusual developments in business and finance, that "extra" on Steel common in late 1923 was news pregnant with meaning to the informed.

In attempting to hit upon leaders in a bull market, the investor should confine his attention to industries of a sound past. Regardless of how favorable temporary circumstances may be, a checkered career signifies a lack of permanent appeal. By now the erratic record, for instance, of sugars, leathers, rubbers, textiles, packers, and the like is so thoroughly recognized as almost to constitute prima facie evidence against such groups enjoying sustained leadership throughout a long major advance. To be avoided as well are the *nouveau riche* or unseasoned, which, like the radio and amusement shares, in their heyday had had no depression test.

Consumer goods stocks—food, clothing, and the like—are usually most responsive to a turn for the better, yet so great is competition and surplus productive capacity as to put a quick blight upon a budding boom. Copper stocks are perennial

American favorites and yet the copper industry is secondary in the sense that the big consumers of copper—electrical equipments—register much earlier the stirrings of business revival and the latter are, for that reason, to be preferred. In just the same manner, steel shares require a pervasive prosperity to manifest a compelling earning power, and, consequently, tend to lag until the late stages of a bull market.

In the long run, the most active stocks—if meritorious—are the safest trading media. General Motors, General Electric, Chrysler, du Pont, Union Carbide, North American, International Harvester, and perhaps a score of stalwart American industrials, will, year in and year out, offer the safest opening for the employment of capital. If top-notch industrials cannot flourish, then it is unlikely that the rank and file of industries can fare better. In the narrow, restricted SEC market of today, salability—which has always been the hallmark of a listed stock—is a major desideratum, as developments since the crash of October, 1937, bear out.

The ideal stock to possess in a major advance is an issue of light capitalization, along with the other requisites of a favorable past and a more promising future. Bethlehem Steel was an example in 1915. Light capitalization means that earnings will pile up rapidly and that the stock, volatile because of limited supply, will respond much more quickly to the influence of rising earnings than would be the case with heavily capitalized companies like Standard Oil of New Jersey, General Motors, Socony-Vacuum, etc.

Another appealing factor is growth or the possibilities of huge expansion. All of these existed years ago in the motors and chain stores and still exist, in all probability, with the chemicals today. Every one may not see the future clearly. The banking firm that guided General Motors through shallow financial waters lost control to W. C. Durant just as the romance of the automobile industry was unfolding. Some imagination, though not too much, is requisite for successful speculation.

CHAPTER EIGHT

The Element of "Romance"

An Example in the Cigarette Industry — Select
Most Promising Industry—Choose Best Individual
Stocks—Technical Reactions

GROWTH is a compelling attribute of the ideal stock in a bull market. It is often described more picturesquely as "romance". Usually all this signifies is that the growth possibilities seem almost limitless for at least several years ahead. Montgomery Ward & Co., Inc., which up to 1927 had been primarily a mail-order house whose prosperity had been roughly measured by farm income, suddenly acquired "romance" when it went into the chain-store business in a big way.

Coming down to a later period, Minneapolis-Honeywell Regulator Co. had "romance" in the big field that existed for temperature control devices for both airconditioning and heating plants. Monsanto Chemical Co., another corporation which multiplied several fold between 1932 and 1937, had—in addition to an impressive background of achievement—"romance" in its room for expansion.

Possible danger in tying up to stocks of this sort, unless the company is large, the record outstanding and finances solid, is the danger inherent in specialties. Any unexpected reversal of fortune or loss of speculative prestige frequently uncovers a thin market, the more palpably in the narrow SEC markets of today. Ordinarily specialty commitments should be weighed carefully.

A good criterion is the possible answer to the old Broadway query about a new show—"Will they buy it?" Logical test of a specialty, therefore, is to ascertain the reactions of half-a-dozen well posted people. If the response of informed judgment is preponderantly negative, the chances are it will be difficult to enlist the speculative following that will make for a satisfactorily broad market.

Choice of individual stocks is fully as important as locating the most promising group. For instance, in the 1933-37 bull market Texas Corp. was the outstanding leader in the oil division, far outstripping the rise in any of the Standard Oil issues which in other oil booms had been the favorites. Not only was Texas Corp. splendidly integrated and with distribution in every state of the Union, but—though operating in most of the important foreign countries—it had no disproportionately large overseas investments at which the stock market could rightfully look askance. Finally, Texas Corp. had a more moderate capitalization for its size than its bigger competitor, Standard Oil Co. of New Jersey. Similarly, Deere & Co. showed a much bigger rise than did International Harvester Co. and for about the same reasons; lighter capitalization and smaller overseas activity.

Another aid in detecting a stock with potentially great prospects in a bull market is to seek an issue in an industry where the so-called secular trend, as measured by annual records, is unmistakably upward. In the 1933-37 bull market Philip Morris was the only outstanding stock in the entire tobacco group. That was because it alone, in a growing industry, was making notable gains.

Time may prove its success to have been a flash in the pan. Certainly the judgment of several of the biggest market operators was wrong in figuring that advertising expenditures would eat up any spectacular profits, as they did for a long time with P. Lorillard Co. when it introduced "Old Gold." The earnings figures of Philip Morris & Co., Ltd., Inc. told a story to which the market gave heed at the same time it was passing by the bigger and more seasoned tobacco equities.

It cannot be emphasized too often, and in this series the statement may be repeated ad nauseam, that earning power—sooner or later—dictates the quotations for individual stocks and for the market as a whole. The rule of thumb used to be that a stock is reasonably priced at 10 times its earning power. If the trend looks clearly upward at the time when a 10-to-1 ratio exists—and other factors essential to a healthy bull market exist— then a stock can be confidently bought.

Of late years the sensational growth of certain industries, notably chemical and aviation, has resulted in a yardstick materially longer than the old-fashioned 10-to-1. As long ago as 1928 John J. Raskob, then chairman of the finance committee of General Motors Corp., publicly went on record that stocks of the caliber of General Motors should sell for "15 times earnings." No hard and fast rule can be set down. Probably somewhere around 15-to-1 is a sound basis for a take-off for a sustained flight.

What is a reasonable capitalization of earning power nowadays is probably the most moot point of discussion in Wall Street. The "biggest and best" issues are here (in the late spring of 1938) selling in many cases for from 30 to 40 times estimated annual earning power. Only the utilities, which are commanding 11 to 12 times earnings ratios, appear reasonably priced. Time alone will tell whether some new and latent influence accounts for the apparently unwarranted price level of the so-called "blue chip" industrial issues. In any event, it is probably safe to say that a group reflecting an old-time market appraisal of earnings is in a buying area, if there is any chance for further improvement.

Certain industries because of their in-and-out erratic performance, namely, the constant recurrence of losses after profits, command a much lower ratio. For that reason sugars, leathers, rubbers, automobile accessories, and the like, are not susceptible to the application of the "times earnings" check. Many investors have been lured to ruin by the superficial appeal of a five or six-to-one earnings ratio which suddenly vanished with the advent of hard times.

Of course, the old saying about a bull market is that "every dog has his day." It is a homely expression which means that in a dynamic bull market speculation broadens out in an engulfing manner to embrace sooner or later nearly every group. Professionals will always attempt to exploit the possibilities of a backward section of the list.

In the present-day system of "managed credit," money assumes a new importance in the field of economics. But while borrowed money is the lifeblood of speculation for the rise, money rates are a much feebler force in determining prices than is generally supposed. In the opinion of the writer extreme money ease cannot of itself generate a bull market, nor, by the same token, can extreme money tension—unless it represents a flagrant abuse of credit facilities—terminate a rise.

The case against the theory that money rates and not earning power are the vital speculative forces has been convincingly expounded in *Interest Rates and Stock Speculation* by Richard N. Owens and Charles O. Hardy, written in 1925 and reissued in 1930 by the Brookings Institution. Instance after instance is therein cited of the lack of correlation between the money market and the stock market. Throughout the latter part of the bull market, in 1928 and 1929, money rates were actually higher than at any time since early 1920.

Research indicates that bull markets usually start before evidence of business improvement. An exhaustive study entitled *Statistical Indicators of Cyclical Revivals,* by Wesley C. Mitchell and Arthur F. Burns of the National Bureau of Economic Research, covering the period from May of 1897 to June, 1932, embracing nine specific cycles, showed that the *Dow-Jones* industrial-share average started up on the average seven months ahead of business. Applying the theory specifically to *Barron's* Business Index and the *Dow-Jones* industrial-share average, it appears that the stock market was ahead of business by four months in the 1908 bull market, one month ahead in the boom of 1918, exactly synchronized in 1932 and about a month ahead in 1933. Since there can be no hard and fast rule, sometimes blind faith is required. If stocks can't go down, they may go up, and the upturn may be forecasting what is invisible on the business horizon.

In the progress of every bull market the ascending price

curve is sometimes interrupted by a sharp downward movement which represents a so-called intermediate correction—what, by some curious twist of phraseology, stock brokers term a "healthy reaction". It usually cancels one-third to one-half of the rise already achieved. It comes about inevitably from the rapid discounting—too quick to be lasting—of favorable factors.

Reversal of a bull trend can be deceptive, for what appears to be a reaction in the major upward movement may turn out to be the first stage of a bear market. To tell the difference is not altogether easy. If the ensuing rally after the reaction is desultory and accompanied by diminution in the volume of transactions, thereby betokening a general unwillingness to bid for stocks at advancing quotations, and if after two or three months prices fail to carry through the previous peak, then careful soundings should be taken.

Again, it makes a difference whether the reaction has occurred only a few months after the apparent start of a bull market. Of course, the inevitable query at this point is "How is it possible to know that a bull market actually has started?" It is never possible to be dogmatic in this respect. Nevertheless, the status of the market and of business just prior to a sustained upward trend is of help in interpreting a reaction. There was, for instance, the collapse of the Repeal Boom in July, 1933. That break occurred after only four months of advance which started after the bank holidays. Obviously there was little to worry about for the long pull in a break that developed four months after a rise out of a condition of banking chaos.

On the other hand, the break which came in the spring of 1937, after an extended upward movement of four years, was a horse of a different color. A serious decline at such a stage calls for utmost wariness. Therefore, the time element is an important factor in determining the significance of an interruption to a broad upward movement.

Other aids in diagnosing the character of a decline are the status of credit and of business inventories. If credit is easy and stocks of goods in the hands of producers are not abnormally high, then the chances are that nothing serious is in the wind. If, however, commercial loans, or brokerage loans, or both, are high, or if inventories by a little investigation prove to have been built up to proportions that only a continued business boom would warrant, then potential menacing sources of liquidation are manifest in the stock market reaction.

Certain technical developments, little straws, are helpful in estimating the strength of an advance. The prompt regaining of its dividend by a stock reflects a healthy demand that has been spurred by the temporary lowering in price when it sells "ex-dividend". Similarly, a good demand for rights, or, to put it another way, the ability of a stock to stand up against the leveling influence of an increase in capitalization reflects a strong, underlying demand.

Split-ups or stock dividends usually occur in the late stages of a bull market. They are brought about by the desire to bring the price down within the range of the average investor's pocketbook and thus to create a broader and better market. In the old days of pools and manipulations, "distribution" of stocks could be effected most easily by lowering the price through a split-up of stock that had got beyond the reach of the average investor or out-and-out speculator. A series of split-ups was often-times the approach to the dénouement of a bull market, the characteristics of which will be set forth a little later.

Pending the crisis that is to usher in a bear market, the nimble-minded investor will not slacken his investigating efforts. He will study income accounts as they appear and deduce therefrom the trend of profits, and, now that sales figures are generally published, the trend of profit margins. The latter are obtained by dividing sales into net income. At the same time, equal attention to balance sheets is necessary to determine the status of inventories and the possible appearance of credit pressure in the shape of bank borrowings.

Waiving aside detailed studies, an easy market approach is zealous watch for signs of waning popularity. If a group or an issue passes out of the zone of activity, and if the transition is accompanied for some time by indecisive price movements or by a downward trend, it is usually warning that forces of deterioration are at work. No need to "reason why" if a stock persists in going against the general trend; the assumption must be that there is something wrong with it.

Despite occasional cross-currents in a bull market, the investor should never lose sight of his main goal. He should retain most of his holdings until the evidence piles up that the sun of a bull market is setting. Always must he resist the passing gusts of changing sentiment.

William M. Wood, for many years head of the American Woolen Co., used to like to relate that in the troubled middle '90s he had at one time made up his mind in favor of a huge commitment in raw wool. The morning of his decision he was greeted by a visitor who portrayed the business outlook in gloomy language which grew gloomier as his visit lengthened. Finally, the temperamental textile head jumped up from his chair and exclaimed, "If you don't mind, I'll have to ask you to get out, for I know that if you stay you will talk me out of $1,000,000 profit." "And," he used to add, "I bought the wool and made the $1,000,000."

Rarely is it profitable to "straddle" in a bull market. The timid or the uncertain quite often are tempted to make a short commitment as a so-called "hedge" against what seems too large or risky a holding. Straddling simply means a diminution of the long position, which could be just as readily done by cutting down its size. In the heyday of a big motor independent, the president—though heavily long of his own stock—every now and then took a flier on the short side of Chevrolet because he just couldn't believe that the soaring price of the unseasoned, Durant-managed motor company could be justified. He was wrong. Chevrolet, lightly capitalized and constantly manipulated, continued to be one of the sensations of that particular bull period.

Speculative decisions involving buying and selling should be clear cut. How successful a firm decision can be may be illustrated by the action of a certain industrialist during the liquor-stock boom of 1933. One of the companies with which he was associated, because of its indirect tie-up with alcohol, suddenly encountered an unreasoning wave of public buying that swept it to levels that were absurd in comparison with any projection of earning power. Without hesitating in the least, he unloaded 50,000 shares of stock in five blocks on a market that literally clamored for more. When the Repeal Boom collapsed, the price of the stock was cut in two and now, five years later, it is dividendless and selling for about one-seventh of what it commanded in the wild days of July, 1933.

Chapter Nine

When to Sell Your Stocks

Human Weaknesses that Prevail at Top—Look Out
for "Easy Riches" Stories—Odd-Lotters Trade
Against Trend—Warning Signals

LOSING a position is the dread of every big-caliber, long-pull
operator. What the fear implies is simply the danger involved in selling too early and of never regaining the original
commitment. Hence wealthy traders, if they attempt to scalp a
profit, make the trial on a comparatively small amount of stock,
on what they call their "trading line." Stock acquired for the
long pull is tenaciously retained.

Here is where an element of psychology enters. It is a
human weakness, that few can overcome, to balk against paying
more for a stock than the price at which it has been sold. Hence
if a stock is sold in the early stages of a bull market, in the hope
of replacement at a lower level, and the market refuses to go
down, the chances overwhelmingly are that—regardless of all
bullish signs—it will not be taken back at a higher price.

Any broker will admit that the unforgivable sin of his calling
is to recommend liquidation at anything short of the absolute
high. Disregarding the inherent optimism of the American
temperament and the extravagant hopes and rumors that flourish
at the top of a bull market, it is the universal resentment against
missing the absolute top of the swing that accounts for the paucity
of selling advices when stocks are churning around at the top.

An easy way of protecting profits at what may prove to have
been the top of a bull market, when the selling recommendations
are so scarce, is to utilize stop-loss orders to conserve profits. If
the general market has been bobbing up and down in somewhat
excited fashion with characteristically high dealings, the odds

are strong that a "blow off" is in the making. It is altogether likely that the most seasoned stocks may be making relatively little progress, though it is possible that a few may be enjoying ascensions. In any event, the situation calls for the clinching of profits through the placement of orders to sell when a given price is reached and that price ought to be a level that has not been violated for several weeks. The utilization of the "sell on stop order" is sound technique in the late, but never in the early stages of a bull market.

But stop losses are only insurance against the sudden culmination of a bull market. Every veteran of Wall Street knows that it is fatal to try to jump in and out of the market. It would take the "seventh son of a seventh son" to catch all the fluctuations. In the narrow SEC-regulated markets, the nimblest of floor traders is as badly hampered as the speculator who never goes near a board room. In any major market movement, play only the big swing.

Avoidance of avarice is almost as vital to success as the inculcation of patience, for the desire for excessive gain is another deep-seated human failing. Always remember that all profits are "paper" until taken and that the market pendulum may some day be swinging in the other direction. Never be thrown off balance by all the fantastic tales of the money that so-and-so may have made, or, more literally, may have "on paper."

There is an old anecdote relating to the exaggeration of easy market gains which runs something like this: An individual remarks to a friend that John Jones has cleaned up a profit of $10,000 on the long side of some issue or other, to which the better informed friend replied, "It wasn't John Jones, it was Jim Black, and he didn't make profit on long side, but on short side. And, as a matter of fact, he took a loss instead of a profit."

It is the story of easy riches that stampedes the uninformed into the market at the top. Brokers know that when the barber and the bootblack are inquiring about the market prices, the dangerous stage is at hand. The mere presence of a horde of the public in the market has always been as pointed a warning of squally weather as a distended brokerage loan account. The "stop, look and listen" warning is usually when a bull market becomes first page news.

Here another bit of advice may be proffered. Never try

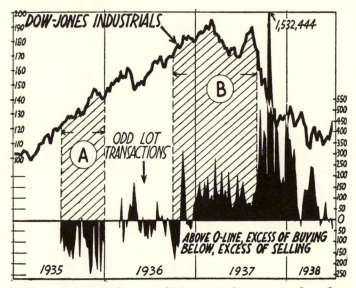

In period A odd-lotters sold 1,300,000 shares more than they bought. In area B they bought 4,600,000 more shares than they sold.

to make the market pay for a definite expense or specific need. Thousands have lost their entire speculative stake in a quick play to pay for taxes, an automobile, a fur coat or something of the sort. The "timing" is almost certain to be wrong. Invariably speculation of that character is impulsive, unreasoning; in reality it is nothing more than gambling.

What the public at large is doing is no longer a mystery. Every day the SEC promptly releases the figures of the odd lot transactions on the New York Stock Exchange of the day before. Toward odd-lot trading, brokers who have been in the businesfor years have a cynical skepticism, based mainly on the evidence that—over the years—the public odd-lot traders have always been wrong.

Whether the Washington authorities believe implicitly in the statement of a former chairman of the SEC that the backbone of security markets has been transferred to the "sticks", is immaterial. Apparently, however, great stress is laid on the odd-lot transactions.

Securities Exchange Commission records of transactions go back to June 7, 1937, just the week before the establishment of the June 14 lows, which represented the first slip of the bear market. As shown by the chart on page 76, however, data are available for several years back. During the first month of the SEC record odd-lots bought heaviest at the low levels of June 14 and 15. Buying on balance continued consistently through July and up to the summer high of August 14. As the market turned downward, buying continued though on a fairly moderate scale. Early in September, however, the pace of buying was rapidly increased, spurted again in mid-September, and also in the final week of that month. Most of this time the market was heading downward.

Now observe what happened on the panic day, Oct. 19, 1937. Biggest daily excess was on the selling side, proving conclusively that hundreds of small traders were forced out. Then bargain hunters appeared. In the two days after the dramatic dip and equally sensational recovery, odd-lots took 1,114,000 shares on balance, or 45% of all the net buying from August 14, date of the midsummer market high. To a student of bull markets the odd-lot operations may be of interest, for certainly the figures show that bargain hunters were out in full force once the news of the panic had been spread throughout the country.

The sequence, however, shows at the time of writing that the odd-lot buying represented no great acumen. The *Dow-Jones* industrial-share average closed Oct. 20, 1937, at 134.56. Little over one month later it was 20 points lower at 114.19.

Eight months later, June, 1938, the averages are still seven points below the Oct. 20, 1937, closing. All of the evidence confirms the long-established professional opinion that "the little fellow is always wrong."

Consider the different manner in which big security holders reacted to the October break. Investment trust reports show these institutions to have been heavy sellers in the final quarter of 1937. Bankers and business men, to whom the market has a message and to whom the memory of the aftermath of October, 1929, is still vivid, immediately began to trim sail. From the date of the October, 1937, market break the big companies almost instantaneously abandoned forward buying on the ground that the following few months would prove whether the stock market was playing its traditional rôle of discounting business adversity not then visible on the horizon.

Business from October, 1937, almost steadily went down hill, the gravity of the inventory problem throughout the country slowly emerged, and the reason for the market slump became all too apparent. To sum up: No matter how cleverly a few individuals may be able to cash in on the automatic rally that always follows a panic, a crash usually is a danger signal instead of a bargain day.

Recall the upheaval that hit Electric Bond and Share in the panic of October, 1929. The leader of the wild utility boom, it was by all odds the most popular individual speculative issue of the period. Originally it had been distributed as a bonus to General Electric shareholders. Its price had multiplied fantastically to the point where hundreds of people almost literally paid it veneration. On the morning of Monday, October 28, Electric Bond and Share opened above 105 and closed at 85; the next morning it opened around 50 a share. In 24 hours the price had been more than halved. What was the sequel?

To be sure, the stock rallied after the establishment of so violent a gap to 117⅝ in 1930, but to help the market price—and inferentially collateral value—the stock only two years later was split back three-for-one. However, today Electric Bond &

Share is selling around $8\frac{1}{2}$, the equivalent of about 3 for the old stock, indicating that the utter collapse in 1929 was no bargain day but a long-term warning.

Long before the underpinnings of a bull market have rotted, a pervasive prosperity has usually flowered into what turns out to be reckless national spending. There was the silk shirt era of 1919, the country club vogue of the 1920's, and the enormous instalment buying by the public in 1937. The rise in commodities, dividends and wages, which are the concomitants of expansion, invariably tend to bring about easy living that ignores the stern law of good times and bad.

Now it may be argued that there was no extravagance prior to the collapse of the Roosevelt boom and that high wages were spent for necessities. More people were enjoying only the proverbial American standard of living. All this may be true, and yet the number of new automobiles on the road—which was a matter of comment by any careful observer in the first half of 1937—indicated that spending was in greater vogue than saving. To expect higher wages and shorter hours and not to have unsoundly high prices was to defy all the laws of economics.

Tendency toward national extravagance is only a superficial sign. What is taking place underneath the business surface is of more real value. No matter how strong may be business activity, no matter how great the momentum of expansion, the possibilities of inventories becoming excessive or of credit accommodations becoming strained must constantly be recognized. Turning away from generalities which may be puzzling to the average investor and getting down to the cause of the 1937 business collapse, the swiftest on record, the only clue available to what was taking place was the subsidence of forward buying all through the summer. Thus, when the period of autumnal business revival occurred in 1937, it took only a further period of subnormal buying to reveal the swollen inventory situation.

Just after the market crash of October, 1937, the writer was in the Middle West, seeking first hand knowledge of what was going on behind the imposing facade of business prosperity.

The purpose was to find out whether the stock market had not discerned breakers ahead, of which Big Business and the New Deal were blissfully ignorant. It took only the first call in Akron, the rubber center, to realize that—in stocking up with goods nine or 10 months previously against the possibility of labor disturbances—business had overplayed its hand. A harassing inventory problem, that was to prove the most serious since 1920, was what was agitating the stock market in the fall of 1937.

Later on, at Chicago, in the course of conversation with the head of one of the biggest merchandising organizations in the country, the query was raised as to the status of inventories. Definite inquiry was made with respect to forward commitments—which are the "contingent liabilities" that can paralyze earnings long after high-priced supplies actually on hand are exhausted. Smiling, the merchandiser replied: "We haven't bought a dollar's worth of goods since the first of last March."

Now that was superb business judgment and the writer expressed that opinion. It is easier to become bearish on stocks at the correct time than on business, especially retail trade, for the latter usually holds up long after the market has turned down.

In answer to the pointed appeal for the formula that so successfully anticipated the future, the statement was, "Nothing magical or mysterious. Come here." Then, turning to a wall chart that pictured the sales curve that ran almost perpendicularly upward, the industrialist added, "Look at that line—straight upward for five years since 1932. No one can expect it to keep on up for 55 years. I decided five years was long enough. No economists told us to quit buying—we don't operate in the higher realms out here."

Another personal incident of the same sort happened in the summer of 1929. Calling on the president of a company, the shares of which were sky-rocketing on the Stock Exchange, the writer opened the conversation with the usual, "What do you know?" Leaning back in his arm chair the man replied, "Well, I've been thinking lately about things. The other day I concluded that all that I knew thoroughly was this business in which I've been ever since school. And what struck me was that this was the first time I could ever recall that there wasn't a cloud on the horizon. So I reasoned 'This can't last' and, for your confidential information, I've sold all of my stock." It didn't take long for his business or market fears to be justified. Within 90 days a price war, for which the industry is notorious, had broken out and the stock in a few months was down 100 points.

Stocks always look best at the top. Realizing that, it is often helpful to look back on the career of a bull market leader. In the summer of 1937 Chrysler stock in some quarters was being labelled an investment issue because of its brilliant earnings and huge dividends forced out by the undistributed-profits tax. Only a minute or two with the record would have shown that in the 1929-32 depression the stock had gone from around $135 to $5 and had returned to the same 1929 high. The chances were overwhelming that the common stock of a company that still had to compete with Ford and General Motors was certainly no investment bargain, regardless of dividends, at close to the highest price in its history.

To be sure, there were hundreds of people who thought stocks were too high in the winter of 1936 but who always ended up by maintaining, "I simply can't sell because of my taxes." Exactly the same excuse ruined some very wealthy people in the terrific deflation of 1920 and 1921. Prices on the Exchange are ultimately determined not by individual tax considerations, but by the trend of earning power. It is better to pay the tax, however much it hurts, than to see the whole paper profit vanish.

Not only forget the tax factor, but also forget all of the gratis advice and enthusiasm prevalent at the top of a big rise. Don't attempt, above all, to lean on anyone. It is necessary to make the individual decision and to suffer the consequences.

Experience may be a dear teacher, but it is the best. It is foolish to rely entirely on one individual or on one service. The public, still believing in the mysterious "they" of Wall Street and Washington and awed by the marble and mahogany of bank and brokerage house interiors, wants to be told what to do. Rather than digest business facts, it swallows "tips".

"Insiders" can never get you out of stocks. You may be "put into" stocks at an advantageous level by some banker or corporate official in a position to know and to appraise a favorable trend of earnings, but you have to get yourself out. Ignorance of this apparently anomalous situation has cost investors too much money not to call for explanation.

Suppose a director or an industrial executive whispers, "I think the stock is too high." The whisper is repeated to a friend, a relative, the broker, and in no time at all—in a district where "grapevine" travels faster than the telegraph—the selling advice is widespread. Pressure on the stock increases, the price weakens steadily. What is the result? Rumors spring up from nowhere concerning the company, its sales, its credit, the quality of its product, etc. Competitors press every advantage. A chance and well-meant remark by a so-called "insider" can conceivably do immeasurable business damage to an industrial concern.

But though "insiders" cannot sound a warning, even if they had clairvoyant judgment—which they signally lacked in 1937—there are certain characteristic and alarming symptoms which prevail when an advance has reached an unhealthy stage.

The most defined characteristics of a climax to a bull market are excessive activity and unhealthy concentration upon inferior stocks. Under the SEC the swirl of dealings at the top may well be less than in the excited markets of the past and, though prophecies are dangerous, certainly nothing like 1929 is likely soon to return. Yet, just prior to the peak of the Roosevelt bull market, March 10, 1937, there had been weeks of abnormally active dealings with 2,000,000 and 3,000,000-share days a commonplace.

So avid was the public appetite for low-priced stocks, all speculative, that both the Stock Exchange and the SEC in turn had to sound warnings. For the reasoning speculator, it is safe to say that the same old danger signal of excessive activity, particularly in low-grade issues, will always function at the top of a bull market.

In conclusion, the best advice for the reluctant seller in a bull market is to consider the working of interest. At 6% compound interest, a calculation which assumes that annual income can continuously be employed at 6%, it takes 12 years for money to double. In the stock market money often doubles within a few months and frequently within a year. Why, then, not be satisfied to have 12 years' growth crammed into a short space of time and sit back and wait for the next period of growth-packing for capital? Why naïvely believe that 12 years' growth of capital can be crammed into a year or less without real danger?

CHAPTER TEN

Bear Markets—"Play No Favorites"

Swiftness and Breadth of Major Declines—Bull
Leaders Become Bear Leaders—Previous Prices
Count for Nothing

A BEAR market is obviously the reverse of a bull market.
Collective preference is for cash instead of securities.
Thus a bear market spells insistent liquidation of stocks and
contraction of liabilities, whereas a bull market is built on increasing demand for stocks and rising liabilities.

Bear markets are anathema because they usher in hard times
for business. Not on falling values and contracting activities
is prosperity reared. Lowered dividends, unemployment, bankruptcies and the like sooner or later appear in a bear market.

Because Americans are perennially optimistic and because
bearishness ultimately reaps such havoc upon the national
economy, bears will always be unpopular in Wall Street. Why
that is so is something for the psychologist to explain. Deliberate refusal to recognize unhealthy market symptoms that may
spell a bear market would seem as foolish as the avoidance of a
doctor when illness threatens.

The out-and-out bear, the prophet of disaster, it would seem,
will always be without honor. Notwithstanding that bear
markets have rolled around with the utmost regularity for the
past 50 years, the threat of liquidation and of lower prices is
always generally decried until it is too late for investors to save
themselves.

If every owner of stocks would only adopt the mental attitude that each and every holding was impermanent, a great deal
of financial anguish would certainly be eliminated. This is not to
imply an abandonment of the policy of riding out a bull market

until recognized, dangerous phenomena appear, but merely to emphasize the futility of believing that any issue can be put away and forgotten. In the very nature of things, bull markets are sure to result in excesses because the tendency in speculation is always for the pendulum to swing too far in one direction or another. A healthy skepticism when the skies are fairest should be part of the endowment of every successful speculator.

It takes brains and courage and a cool head to be a good bear. Almost anyone in good health and funds can be a bull. The most casual knowledge of business or of economic history reveals how regularly bad times succeed good and how severe depressions can be. It is the stubborn belief that everything is for the best in the United States that has carried thousands of investors to their ruin. Most people can recall the smugness prevalent in the financial district throughout 1929 and almost everyone in the country knows how certain were the New Dealers in the fall of 1936 in the solidity of managed prosperity. Widely scoffed at were those who first questioned the underpinnings of the Hoover and Roosevelt booms.

The result of excessive, ingrained optimism is that a change from good times to bad is so great a shock as usually to paralyze investment decision. The chief characteristic of a bear market is its swiftness. Like a bolt from the blue comes the first wave of selling that launches a genuine or major liquidating market. One day all is serene; a week or two later panic may rage. That was the story in 1929 and it was duplicated in 1937. In a few weeks the laborious upbuilidng of values for months was wiped out.

A true story may illustrate the dual point of how rapidly prices may crumble with the advent of a bear market and how impossible it is for those with over-extended commitments to make adjustment. In 1929 the great indoor sport of a comparatively little known mid-western industrialist, whose entire fortune lay in common stocks, was to add up each night after the closing his net worth "on paper." By millions his stockmarket equity rose, until at last his computation in the late summer reached the magical figure of $100,000,000. Soon after came a smash in motor and automobile-accessory stocks, both of which —having made their highs earlier in the year—should have served warning to the westerner that Wall Street was no longer a one-way street. By the spring of 1930 (in less than a year) the man who considered himself worth $100,000,000 was obliged to ask for an extension of time for the payment of assessments on failed banks in which he was a heavy stockholder.

The other salient characteristic of a bear market is its encompassing breadth. First one group descends perpendicularly as the general market tumbles. Then, as prices rally and steady after the panic, certain groups appear to be impregnable. As the months drag on, however, and the grim realities of what the initial break was discounting emerge, the apparently impregnable sections of the list give ground. Necessitous selling is no respecter of stocks and price stability simply invites liquidation.

Therefore, because bear markets are so swift and, before their completion, so all-encompassing, the first rule in a bear market is to discard manuals, reports and data of all description. Only by subscribing to the thesis that all stocks fall together in a bear market can serious losses be avoided. Few individuals there are who do not in a bear period cling, to their sorrow, to some "pets" in the mistaken notion that their particular issues can escape the effects of the wholesale liquidation.

There is an obvious exception to the rule of "Never buy in a bear market (except in the late stages)" and gold stocks are the classic example. In recognition of the likelihood that deflation would upset the old gold standard, gold stocks started up in 1933 and made consistent progress throughout the Roosevelt bull market. And then there are certain "defensive" stocks that can be benefited by deflation, as witness in 1937-38 the experience of Corn Products Refining Co., the earnings of which were sharply reversed by the sharp decline in corn prices.

Of course, all stocks don't move down at once any more than they rise together in a bull market. General Electric, for instance, made its high in 1930, long after the market crash. Oil stocks in the fall of 1937 seemed immune to depression and yet, before the spring of 1938, inventories had reached record-breaking proportions, prices had softened and earnings were declining to an extent that brought in effective selling. Worst of all speculative weaknesses is to put a halo around any stock or group of stocks.

Actual trading for the fall has been greatly restricted as compared with former years. The Federal Reserve Board demands 50% margins, as against 40% for purchases. It insists that short sales can be executed only at prices higher than the previous quotation. In calculating the value of brokerage accounts, there is the same barrier against pyramiding on the short side as there is on the long side. The result is that it is impossible to "force the going" in order to break prices down rapidly by short selling and thereby to bring about convulsive liquidation on the order of 1929-32. For these reasons the tempo of the advanced stage of bear markets may become much slower than in the past.

For the business man facing a period of retrenchment and curtailed profits, short selling in the stock market is nothing more than a "hedge" against adversity. The short seller alone cannot force down prices—certainly he cannot under the new rule. Only the fundamentals that dictate major movements can bring that about. Hence, the little minority of short sellers—who are able to rid themselves of haunting memories of an occasional "corner" or two—are entitled to the reward that the active can always wrest from the "do nothings."

It is an ironical fact, probably based on the law of action and reaction, that the leaders of a bull market turn out to be the leaders of the ensuing bear market. When general enthusiasm for certain stocks has become so great as to establish fancy figures, a top-heavy situation is created which becomes vulnerable to selling. As each new price stratum is reached, new liquidating forces are set in motion that—because of the widespread ownership—feed upon themselves.

Not only were the utilities sensations of the 1924-29 bull era and leaders of the 1929-32 bear market but also conditions had so radically changed as to make them fresh victims of the 1937-38 bear market. One only has to contrast the high-water marks for utilities in 1937 with the peak of 1929 to see what can happen to the favorites of yesteryear.

The original bear leader of 1929 always sought out by careful questioning of brokerage houses throughout Wall Street where the big public "long" positions lay. No violation of ethics occurred in securing such information. Floor brokers are usually able to "smell out" an unwieldy public long interest and the mere gossip of the marketplace usually reveals the public favorites.

On these issues in 1929 the bear operator concentrated his initial selling activities. Consolidated Gas was first choice because it was so heavily carried on margin. Today there are cynics who aver that in lieu of large public positions, short selling that carries the least hazard may well be directed against the big lines held by investment trusts which are the conscious or unconscious victims of the enthusiasm rampant at the top of a bull market.

So-called "inventory" stocks are extreme sufferers in a major bear movement. Therefore, while it may be sound advice to discard the manuals and statistics, it is well to study inventory positions. In a sharp business deflation—whether of volume or of prices, or both—big inventories are proportionately as great a liability to corporations as they are an asset in a period of business activity and rising prices. Rubber and sugar equities were almost erased in 1920 and 1921.

What are the signals of an impending bear market? Naturally the phenomena are those that accompany the culmination of a bull market: excessive activity, exploitation of inferior stocks, tendency toward national extravagance of living, belief that prices cannot go down (witness the "New Era" of 1929 and "Inflation" in 1937), and rampant optimism. In addition to all these factors, there is usually some very clear-cut warning, the significance of which not long afterwards appears unmistakable.

In 1929 as high an authority as the British Chancellor of the Exchequer, Philip Snowden, inveighed against Wall Street speculation in the following terms: "There must be something wrong, something which needs attention, when an orgy of speculation in a country 3,000 miles away should dislocate the financial system here and inflict grave suffering upon workers in practically every country in the world. This is a matter to which our serious attention must be directed."

In the spring of 1937 President Roosevelt, in whose hands inflationary powers lay, declared that commodity prices were too high and struck out sternly against steel and copper prices. Alert speculators will always be on the lookout for what may be "warnings" along the uncertain market road.

Such statements from "high quarters" especially in 1937 carried greater weight because of the action taken just two months previously by banking authorities to arrest the progress of an allegedly unhealthy boom. For, on January 30, 1937 the Federal Reserve Board increased the reserve requirements against demand and time deposits of member banks, thereby sharply reducing the volume of excess credit. At the time such banking measures are always interpreted as precautionary, but the sequel is inevitably deflation.

Once a bear market gets under way it is necessary, above all, to remember that *previous prices count for nothing*. The stock market is always discounting an entirely new set of circumstances. If the odds, for instance, are staked heavily against the railroads, it makes no difference whether New York Central has sold in the past at 200 or 300, or any figure that might be named. If new factors are at work it is possible for the solid railroad equities to be wiped out entirely, as they were in the railroad reorganization period of the '90s. Failure to recognize that previous prices count for nothing has probably kept more people from selling stock than any single influence.

It is only fair to say that "previous prices count for nothing" is just as true of a bull as of a bear market. A stock can start from scratch, which is to say, from as low as even $1 a share, and go anywhere if the factors are propitious. The reorganized railroads of the 1890's, Union Pacific and Atchison, became the premier investments in the boom that led up to the 1907 panic. "Romance" of the type of electric refrigeration, airconditioning, aviation and the like, can conceivably remove possibility of any pre-determined price ceiling. However, the tax power of the Government, as revealed in the tendency in Great Britain and the United States, is to penalize localized, new and abnormal prosperity.

Then there is that insidious investing weakness of a bear market, viz., "averaging". Never average on a stock that has declined. The chances are 99 to 1 that at the time of the contemplated new purchase there are more attractive opportunities elsewhere. In any event, as no buying should be done in a bear market, "averaging" is obviously unsound.

It is well known that the market difficulties years ago of W. C. Durant arose from "averaging". In his case the operations were of so large a nature as to constitute support. Support—or "pegging"—in a bear market simply invites liquidation. The writer has seen the one-time famous auto magnate buy block after block of General Motors in a single day, only to have the price close lower.

The penetration of pivotal points—50, 75 or 100—for example, always used to be in old-fashioned bear markets the signal for the outbreak of convulsive liquidation. Tendency of the public has always been to put in buying orders at a round price so that, once that price is violated and buying power eliminated, prices tumble rapidly.

In 1929 one of the leading bear figures of that period was conducting a big bear operation in Montgomery Ward. He had been selling it rather liberally in the lower 50's when the suggestion was sent up from the floor of the Stock Exchange that he "cease firing" because of the huge support that prevailed at 50. In answer to his query "What 'support'?" word came back "between 30,000 and 40,000 shares." In 15 or 20 minutes streams of Montgomery Ward appeared on the tape and in short order the stock had broken 50. Just before closing time, the same stock, which at 1 o'clock was selling around 52, was commanding in the neighborhood of 43—a $9 break in less than two hours. In short, just as soon as all orders were filled at the pivotal point, the stock broke almost $7.

Nowadays with professionals banned or withdrawn from the market, the breaking of a pivotal figure is not followed by so rapid a decline. Chrysler, favorite of the public for years, has gone below 50 several times without a swift collapse. On the other hand, an investment stock like American Telephone lived up to all the predictions of well-posted specialists and odd lot houses by breaking almost 13 points in 1938 once it went under the quasi-magical figure of 140.

Because bear markets are encompassing and because it is always futile to buck a trend, it is well when liquidating to sell "at the market." Too many huge losses have resulted from quibbling over fractions. Let the broker who has the order do the worrying. The only real danger in strict adherence to selling "at the market" is in the event of an overnight break. As a general thing, the stock market abhors a gap as does Nature a vacuum. The tendency is for professional speculators to look for a rise where changes are stunningly abrupt. Therefore on a widely lower opening it is usually the better part of wisdom to wait at least an hour or two for the so-called automatic rally that comes in the wake of panicky liquidation.

The writer is reminded of an individual who decided to sell his holdings of American Smelting in the summer of 1937 when the stock was around 95. The first 500 shares were sold at a decline of about $\frac{3}{4}$ point; then 200 shares were disposed of at a concession of a full point. Word was then flashed back from the floor of the Stock Exchange that the nearest bid was $1\frac{1}{2}$ points away and "Unless the stock has to be sold today, why not wait for a better bid in the morning?" Instead of a better bid next morning, the stock opened off $2 a share. For procrastination and for not selling "at the market" the penalty was a loss of over $1,000 on the 500 shares that remained to be liquidated.

At the first sign of trouble the investor should weed out his poorest stocks. It is a well known fact that the public acts contrariwise. It invariably sells the best stocks and holds on to the poorest. The reason for this is that the weak stocks break badly and the average trader is loath to sacrifice paper profits or to accept a loss.

Willingness to take a loss is absolutely vital to success. No one can be right forever. Business men guess wrong on prices or styles and have to pay the piper. Acceptance of a small loss may free capital for a better undertaking and cut short losses that can develop into an appalling shrinkage.

"Always guard against synthetic optimism," should be the slogan of every realist in a bear market. Memory of the Hoover utterances is still green and "prosperity just around the corner" is a classic jest. Politicians and bankers and big business men probably will always persist in the belief that the gospel of optimism can arrest a depression. All that unwarranted optimism does is to postpone the evil day or to provide a "breathing spell" deceptive to investors.

When the heavy guns of cheerful publicity are unloaded from the captains of finance or politics, it is always well to be on guard. Only the fundamentals of business activity and earning power can stem a bear market. Usually the blasts of optimistic propaganda emanate before the initial break in a bear market has occurred and invariably long before the decline has culminated. In the Hoover Administration cheerful comments became a joke before 1932 rolled around.

CHAPTER ELEVEN

Three Stages of a Bear Market

Beware of Technical Rallies—Watch Market as
a Whole—Bull Factors Become Bearish—How
Bear Markets End

IF an active policy is undertaken in a bear market, stocks
to be chosen are not only those which have enjoyed a concentrated and possibly abnormal degree of prosperity but also issues
with a large capitalization. Breadth of market must always
be sought in operating for the fall or rise—but particularly for
the fall. Experienced speculators know this only too well and
always make sure of being able to "turn around" at any time
without a disastrous penalty. In stocks with a narrow market
the trader may almost put prices up or down by his own purchases
or sales.

At the outset, seasoned investment issues are slowest to
decline. This is because of their intrinsic strength which only
the steady erosion of a depression can undermine. It is in the
late stages of a bear market, when individuals and institutions
have to sacrifice holdings, that the conventional investment
issues cave in.

While invariably swift, a bear market is not the easy road to
riches that it might appear. At some stage occurs a sharp technical rally that is perhaps the most deceptive of all market phenomena. It arises chiefly from the fact that a liquidating movement, as it progresses, spreads apprehension and brings in so
concentrated and convulsive a selling movement as to result in
a too rapid levelling of values. Although the destruction of capital consumes a shorter space of time than the upbuilding, it is
nevertheless possible for liquidation temporarily to over-reach
itself. In other words, somewhere or other a bear market finds

itself in the position of having discounted adversity too far ahead.

Business men and investors who can see nothing on the horizon to warrant the sudden collapse of values and who refuse to take stock in the significance of a crash, prove willing buyers. Then if the short interest is excessive with relation to the floating supply of stock, which is to say, to the amount of stocks in purely speculative hands, the stage is set for the so-called technical rally. For the most part, only speculative sophisticates are familiar with the development and only they need be concerned with it, since for the rank and file of traders the part of wisdom is to defer buying until the characteristic evidences of the culmination of selling occur.

Danger of this technical rally lies in the tendency of security holders to overlook the significance of the preceding decline. At this stage of a bear market business is usually good and the surface appearance of earning power is all that could be desired. There is a renascence of optimism, and from all sides comes the traditional cry that the market break was only an interruption in an incomplete period of expansion. In early 1930 and again in late 1937 the statement was repeatedly made that the market decline had been so rapid as to represent a satisfactory corrective and not for some weeks did disillusionment occur.

Exhaustion of the technical rally is usually to be detected in a gradual tapering off in the volume of transactions and failure of prices to mount higher.

Another clue to the ebbing of vitality of the market's technical rally is a lack of breadth, manifest by the failure of representative groups to participate. Frequently only one or two stocks may be making important progress on the upside while the market as a whole is merely churning around. The slightest faltering of a recovery—after a preliminary crash—should be regarded with extreme apprehension and as a selling spot for those who may not have got out before the first downswing.

Even the best of speculators can go wrong while a technical

rally is flourishing. Here's an example: In the late spring of 1930 a colossal speculation for the rise was being conducted by the 1929 bull leader in General Electric. The stock, which had been split up, was selling in the low 90's. Now the operator in question was not only the biggest speculator that ever came into Wall Street, but he had a following of the most formidable proportions from the wealthiest capitalist to the humblest waiter. It was difficult for the most hardboiled bear to resist the arguments of the famous bull leader.

On that particular day in 1930, so magical was his name and so tremendous his legion of followers that he had been actually able to dispose, after the close of the Stock Exchange, of several 25,000-share lots of General Electric to three of the biggest capitalists in the country. One would have thought that the Exchange would not be open the following morning. Remember that this all took place in the days before the SEC. At an uptown hotel the same evening, the bull leader stressed his success in selling stock "off the board and after the close" and his confidence in the ability to push the stock to 125.

As he talked with increasing conviction and vehemence he succeeded in securing several big buying orders for the opening the next day. Swayed by the talk, a confirmed bear—who had remained unmoved by all the eloquence—suddenly ejaculated "OK, put me down for 40,000 shares in the morning." At that point a friend kicked the speaker beneath the table and, leaning over, whispered "Watch your step, I've never heard such wild bullish talk in my life." In a split second the wary bear operator leaned over and whispered back, "Never mind, you sell through your son, who is on the floor, 80,000 shares in the morning." In other words, the big bear had quickly converted his 40,000-share bull position into a 40,000-share short position. The story is told not for the purpose of reciting the fantastic market exploits of that foolish era, but to illustrate the quickness and flexibility of judgment requisite for successful speculation, and, incidentally, to illustrate the deceptiveness of technical rallies.

The pitting of bear against bull, as thus outlined in the anecdote concerning General Electric in 1930, is the epitome of fact against wishful thinking. The bear operator, temporarily swept off his feet, came back to solid mooring on his earlier conviction that a major depression—in which even General Electric could not escape—was under way. The bull, impressed by the current brilliant earning power, refused to look ahead to what might be taking place a few months hence.

One of the oldest of axioms is "Never sell a dull market." The adage was meant to apply, however, to bull markets, since it signified a lack of liquidating pressure and the implied presence of stocks in strong hands. A rally in a bear market, when accompanied by dullness, signifies a general unwillingness on the part of investors to follow up advancing quotations, or, in other words, a lack of dynamic force in the recovery. Following the spring break of 1937, the quiet markets of the ensuing summer—in which there was not a single 2,000,000-share session from May through August while prices moved back almost to the previous peak—were a case in order, and so was the dullness following the January, 1938, rise.

In brief, volume is the best evidence of dynamic power. If activity picks up on the decline, the presumption is that liquidating forces are being set in motion as prices fall. If an impasse prevails, declining quotations would not bring in an increase in offerings.

It is never profitable to "quarrel with the tape," and one must believe that the "market can do anything." Who could possibly have believed, prior to the New Deal, that mere "bigness" in a corporation might prove a liability? "Growth" and "size" were the big bull arguments of 1928 and 1929.

The writer is here reminded of some sage comment proffered him, long before the devastating depression of 1929-32 was far advanced, by the head of a flourishing independent motor company. Talking with him in his Detroit office one afternoon, the subject turned to the fierce competition that smaller units had to encounter at the hands of the biggest companies in their field. Smiling grimly the motor executive said, "We're doing our best, though probably the 'Big Three' are bound to get us eventually. But let me tell you, the American public some day will attack business on size alone and I think I can even see the handwriting on the wall for chain-store companies." How prophetic that comment was may be found from the subsequent record of punitive chain-store taxation throughout the country and the bills offered in Congress that would—if enacted—virtually confiscate chain-store businesses.

In a bear market where the pace may be leisurely and where volume signs may be lacking, there are certain technical indications which, reversing the messages in a bull market, are ominous. Failure of individual stocks promptly to regain dividends, after having sold "ex" dividend payment, is an unhealthy manifestation. Another significant sign is a decline in price following the announcement of fresh financing. Inability both to recover a dividend and to resist the diluting effects of new financing reflects a situation where demand is weak.

It cannot be too constantly emphasized that the clarion call of a bear market is the first real break. It constituted the clear-cut warning in October, 1929. The mild decline of March-June, 1937, was ominous though much less emphatic. Coming in both instances after years of rising prices, the message should have been clear to the open-minded investor. It is easy at the time to maintain that the slaughter of prices was an accident but as well-known a bear operator as Jesse Livermore used to say, "such accidents are usually along the line of least resistance." To add emphasis to the point, Livermore would say "Never try to do all your selling at the top."

On the other hand, nothing is more unprofitable than premature buying. Late in 1930 United States Steel common, having virtually halved its 1929 high, was selling around 135. A friend, meeting the then-famous leader of the powerful bear clique, remembered that a western banker had said "I'm putting my last dollar into Steel common when it hits 100." Of this the ruthless bear operator remarked, "He'll get his stock, all right, and he'll get a headache with it." Less than two years later Steel common was selling in the low twenties, 75% below the assumed "buying level" of 100.

Another story may illustrate that a swift decline is not the end of a market readjustment but possibly an early phase of a long-drawn-out reversal of values. Back in the 1929-32 bear market, one of the handful of big-calibered operators sold 10,000 shares of Allied Chemical short around 250, which was over 100 points under the 1929 peak. In due course, he covered at 100 points profit, netting $1,000,000. But so easily accomplished was the process of covering, that he immediately again went short though at a lower level of 10,000 shares and subsequently covered at nearly the same profit.

Lest such glamorous stories divert the attention of the average trader from the character of bear markets, it may be pertinent to point out a curious anomaly related to the thesis that leading stocks in bear markets are usually the leaders of the previous bull market. The anomaly is that prior bullish factors frequently are double-edged. What was bullish during the rise may carry a bearish meaning in the decline.

The "leverage" factor, so potent in the rise of utilities in the 1920's, was a serious burden in the following depression. The heavy volume of senior securities, which made equities so "thin" that earnings leaped forward as sales expanded, was a tremendous incubus on profits as sales contracted. More lately, the undistributed-profits tax, which forced out huge dividends in 1936 and 1937, necessitated conservation of working capital and, consequently, rapid contraction of payments in the early months of 1938.

Since it is insisted constantly to follow the main trend and since the advice has been given to discard figures in a bear market, beware of abnormally large yields or startlingly low capitalization of earning power. A high yield rarely lasts long and is often suddenly explained by the actual cessation of payments. A low capitalization of earning power, which is to say, a small ratio of price to per-share balances, usually reflects water that has gone over the dam. The splendid earnings of 1937 were no index to the results of the early months of 1938—all of which is explained by the fact that speculation never looks backward but always forward.

Unseasoned bears are sometimes rendered apprehensive by what veterans regard as minor irritants. The payment of a "premium" for borrowing a stock in which the short interest may be temporarily congested and payment of dividends when stocks sell "ex-dividends" are discouraging to the rank and file. In reality they are no more than the interest or the "carrying charge" incurred in a bull market.

"Where the risk is greatest the profit is greatest" says one of the most astute and unemotional bear traders of all time. Merely because a stock had universal esteem never deterred him from selling it if a study of the fundamentals proved it vulnerable.

There are three stages to a bear market. The first is the initial stunning decline in quotations. The second is the steady sag induced by the exposure of poor business and poor earnings. The final leg is the gruelling process wherein stocks are sold to meet pressing cash needs and where the stark nakedness of the depression is exposed in the form of bankruptcies, receiverships, suspended dividends, and the like.

The culmination of a bear market, as might be supposed, is exactly the opposite of the dénouement of a bull market. A long period of agonizing dullness, in which stocks move in a narrow range, is the surest indication of the exhaustion of liquidating forces and the conclusive evidence is usually the refusal—after a period of languishing markets—of stocks to go down in the face of bad news.

Stock traders, or investors, if you will, should never live in a fool's paradise. Paper profits are never tangible until realized. The tragedy is that it takes a bear market to drive the fact home. To the myriads to whom parting with a favorite stock is akin to divorce it is well to point out the hackneyed statement that "the market is always here tomorrow". The elder John D. Rockefeller is reported to have told a persistent seeker for a tip on Standard Oil of New Jersey, "I think it will fluctuate."

CHAPTER TWELVE

The Pattern in Bear Markets

Influence of Investment Trusts—Changes in Investment Preference—Logical Sales in Bear Market

BEAR markets of the future, in all probability, will present a different pattern from those of the past, by virtue of the radical new rules of the Securities and Exchange Commission that now govern speculation. Since early February, 1938, short sales in round lots have been permissible only at a price above the last sale and since late May the odd lots have come under the same ban. The new rules did not prevail during the dynamic phase of the 1937-38 bear market in the fall of 1937. In fact, barring the spill in the closing days of March, 1938, no long sustained liquidating movement has to date taken place under the new régime.

What the new regulations spell is an inability of professional bears to press an advantage. In the old days, once a selling movement was launched, it was possible to accelerate its momentum by pressing stocks for sale "at market", regardless of price. By unloading large lots at typical resistance levels, which are even figures like 50 or 100 for individual stocks, a demoralizing selling movement could be mechanically initiated. Hereafter the bears will have to wait on the advent of genuine selling.

By the same token, it is probable that when a bear market, lacking a substantial short account, gets under way, the technical position will be so weak as to be without an important buying cushion. It is a falling market that gives bears confidence in selling short. Hence when selling breaks out the market will lack the stabilizing force of a short interest, which, as it constantly covers, tends to bring about temporary stability or even sharp rallies.

Thus it would seem as though selling, both long and short, will have to be undertaken for the longer pull and be conducted coldly and unemotionally. It may be too late to get rid of large lines of stock once the first significant little decline makes its appearance. Perhaps in the long run all this may be for the best, inasmuch as few markets are so dominated by emotional thinking as the Stock Exchange.

Another new influence—assuming its potentialities are not modified—is that of investment trusts, now the reservoirs of big common stock holdings. Investment trust ownership has tended enormously to cut down the floating supply of stocks and thereby to make for more rapid price fluctuations. Investment trust managers are as human as anybody else and are prone to be influenced by psychology. Unless a policy is adopted on the part of investment trusts of scale operations, i. e., buying and selling on an ascending and descending scale against the main trend, the attempt to sell or buy big blocks will have an abnormally sharp influence on quotations.

An important reason why short selling has always been unpopular with the public is not alone that it runs contrary to ingrained American optimism, but because of the fear engendered by the remembrance of occasional spectacular "corners". The sensational Northern Pacific corner of 1901, when during the battle of the Harriman and Hill forces for control the stock shot to 1,000, from 160, can be recalled by old-timers. The memory of the Stutz "affair" in 1920, when the stock of the now defunct motor company rose to 391, from 100¾, is still fresh in the memory of the older speculators. Place on top of such occurrences the new artificial market status brought about by SEC rules, investment trust operations and the banning of insider transactions, and it is easy to visualize a bear market in which the most rabid pessimist will be loath to operate for the decline.

For the present generation of investors and speculators the course of the 1937-38 bear market is probably the most interesting to follow. The first phase was a decline of almost 29 points in a little over three months, March 10 to June 14, 1937. The natural query is: How could anyone know that the break was to initiate a bear market, especially when in the following two months the market recovered 25 points to sell within $4\frac{1}{2}$ points of its March high?

The answer is that no one could be dogmatically sure. But after a rise of four years from Feb. 26, 1933, during which the *Dow-Jones* industrial-share average almost quadrupled from a low of 50.16, the chances were—on the time element alone—in favor of the decline being a precursor of a long downward movement. In three years alone prior to March 10, 1937, had occurred an almost uninterrupted rise during which the industrial-share average had doubled. It was time to be on the lookout for the unexpected.

Then in the late summer, when—if a bull market still prevailed—preparations to discount seasonal business improvement in the fall should have been taking place, came another lurch which carried prices below their previous lows. The second decline was the sharpest of warnings of the existence of a bear market.

With the second warning came the dynamic phase of the bear market. Prices sank gradually until mid-October, when a full-fledged panic prevailed with stocks breaking wide open and the volume of trading soaring above the 7,000,000-share mark. In the single week of October 18-23, over 22,000,000 shares of stock changed hands. Panics are always followed by temporary, automatic recoveries, and, true to precedent, came a rally the following week of about 13 points. Less than a month later stocks were down 25 points to another new low. The autumn months brought the workings of the big forces of liquidation.

After the violent fall break ensued a gradual recovery featured by the conventional January rise which carried within four points of the peak of the "automatic rally" that followed the October panic. Then came a see-saw movement through February, followed by a fresh break in the closing days of March when the *Dow-Jones* industrial-share average broke practically 16 points. Note, here, however, that less than 8,000,000 shares changed hands in the five days of violent selling.

Little over two weeks later the market was up 22 points, an indication of powerful resistance to the forces of liquidation. Thereafter speculation fell into the doldrums. Five weeks of intense dullness set in. The stage was thus set for a reversal of prices, which, in a buying movement of stupendous proportions, lifted the industrial-share average in two weeks by over 25 points.

The bear market of 1929-32, most disastrous on record, was quite different. To begin with, it lasted two years and eight months, as compared with some 12 months for the 1937-38 movement. For a rough rule of thumb, bear markets usually run from one year to one and a half years. A period of liquidation extending beyond 18 months or so usually betokens an extraordinary set of circumstances, such as prevailed in the greatest world-wide depression on record, 1929-32.

The first phase of the 1929-32 bear market came in the break from the high of Sept. 3, 1929, of 381.17 for the *Dow-Jones* industrial-share average to 198.69 on November 13. On one single day, October 29, the volume of trading ran as high as 16,410,000 shares, and on another the tape ran over four hours late at the close.

Then came the most deceptive recovery that has probably ever been witnessed on the New York Stock Exchange, a rally of over 95 points to 294.07 on April 17, 1930. Though spread over a much longer period, it corresponded to the compressed rally of June-August, 1937.

In the spring of 1930 prices see-sawed for a month or two and then worked gradually down through the summer and fall, until on Dec. 16, 1930, some 15 months after the 1929 peak, a new low was reached at 157.51, well below the first bottom of November, 1929. The following year, 1931, was dismal; 1932 worse, and not until July 8 of that year did prices bottom. Though for so extended a bear market no precedent exists, yet, who is to say that some time or other another liquidation as prolonged as that may not take place?

Going back to 1919 one finds more resemblance to the disconcerting bear market of 1937-38. Prices had hit their

highs, 119.62, in November of 1919 in the post-armistice inflationary boom. First bottom came 30 points lower, Feb. 25,
1920, followed by rally to April 8. On May 19 prices penetrated
the February low, sending up the second warning of a bear
market, but, unlike 1937, violent liquidation did not get under
way until late fall. The industrial-share average stayed in the
middle 80's until early November. In December the averages
broke to 66.75. Although the exact bottom of the bear market
was not touched until Aug. 24, 1921, at 63.90, the bear market,
it can be seen, had really spent itself in a little over a year.

Now there are some marked differences in the characteristics
of these three bear markets which account for their different
performances. In 1937-38 the irritant was an extended inventory
position, nothing more nor less. There was no commercial or
speculative loan structure to be liquidated. In 1929-32 there
were enormous speculative and commercial credit structures
to be razed the world over. In 1919-21 there was the inventory
problem, but no formidable debt structure to be torn down.
The strong factor in 1919-21 was the surplus fat of war prosperity
retained by corporations, still to be fried out in the form of
dividends. On the latest occasion, 1937, there was the tremendous influence of managed, easy money. Anyone studying
fundamentals should be able to see why the 1919 and 1937 bear
markets were short and swift.

Bear markets are fascinating to the avaricious because
money is made so quickly, but let no one think that even bear
leaders cannot be misled by the ease with which prices can be
knocked down. In the early summer of 1932 the famous bear
coterie of that time was pounding United States Steel common
and privately telling friends that the stock would sell "down
around the figure for Radio." Radio Corp. of America was then
selling for about $4 a share and United States Steel was in the
middle 20's. Every afternoon toward the close the bears would
"turn on the heat" to bring about the break in price which,
reflected in the closing quotation, would influence thousands of
people.

It soon began to be noticeable, however, that liquidation did not follow in the wake of the bear maneuvers. The fact was that the bear market had about run its course. Steel common, instead of joining Radio, more than trebled in price in just over a year. The bears in 1932 had simply forgotten the time element, just as the bulls had in 1929 and 1937. After $2\frac{2}{3}$ years of decline to July, 1932, a turn of the tide was bound to be close at hand.

Another story will illustrate how corrosive may become the philosophy of pessimism. Early in 1933, when alert speculators first began to recognize the speculative potentialities of gold shares, a famous bear took a number of friends to the "Lake District" of Canada. There some of the best Canadian gold mines were inspected. When it came time to return from the gold mining district to the States, the host of the party suggested a visit to the International Nickel properties.

Several guests, anxious to return to their desks, demurred at staying longer, but some of the impatient were told that the trip would be worthwhile in order to see the "greatest white elephant on the western hemisphere," i. e., the famous Frood mine in Ontario. International Nickel, then selling at $9 a share, was in complete disrepute. Yet it was to turn out to be the international investment favorite in the following five years and the steadiest mining issue on the New York Stock Exchange throughout the 1937-38 bear market. The moral of the story is that after a tremendous bull or bear market it is imperative that one acquire the perspective of a commonsense approach to values and to disregard the figures and conditions of the moment.

Just as women's hats reveal glaring changes in feminine styles, it takes a bear market to bring about changes in investment preferences. Measured solely by activity, studies show that the railroad stocks were the favorite dividend-payers in 1901, but by 1910 had begun to slip in favor of industrials and utilities. By 1919 only two rails were among the 20 most active dividend-paying stocks, with the "war brides" dominating the list. By 1926 motor issues overshadowed all others. Utilities and metals outweighed all groups for 1929 and in 1937 metal and chemicals predominated. A record of 40 years' style changes in investments shows how vital and important flexibility is for success in the handling of securities.

Of late years investment trust portfolios have reflected the fashion of the day. Just contrast 1933 with 1937. In the earlier

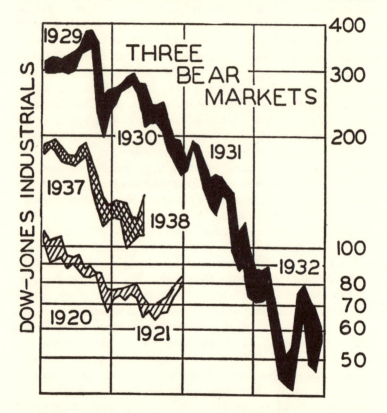

period the three most popular stocks were General Motors, American Gas & Electric and du Pont. Four years later the three most popular were International Nickel, Texas Corp. and Standard Oil of New Jersey—the first two being newcomers. Between 1933 and 1937 du Pont, J. C. Penney, three railroads—

Chesapeake & Ohio, Pennsylvania and Union Pacific, two utilities—Public Service of New Jersey and Pacific Gas & Electric, Standard Oil of California and Liggett & Myers had disappeared from the list of the 15 most popular. While investment trusts can err badly, as the records show, portfolios pretty well reflect the rise and ebb of investment favor.

In an out-and-out bear market the stocks which logically should suffer the most are those with big inventories or big borrowings, or both, though borrowings in a period of abnormal money ease may be glossed over. Marginal producers in any field—copper, oil, steel and the like—will suffer. The so-called "leverage" stocks, where a heavy volume of fixed charges is an onerous burden on profit margins in a competitive business period, will necessarily shrink rapidly. Among seasoned investments a demonstrated lack of secular growth, which means a receding total business volume for the industry concerned, is something to watch out for. And, finally, there is the all-encompassing political factor that of late years has raised havoc with the utility and chain-store issues.

Though no species is more unpopular in Wall Street than the bear, it is necessary for security traders to recognize that bear markets will follow bull markets, just as hard times follow good. Try as industry and Government may, it is doubtful if the business cycle, or what foreign economists term "Konjunktur", can be erased.

Keep in mind that bear markets are swift and stunning and will probably be difficult to capitalize hereafter. That makes all the more imperative the search for the signs of the culmination of a bull market: big activity, widespread prosperity and careless national spending habits. Realize also that the only recognizable characteristic of the termination of a major liquidating movement on the Stock Exchange is a period of agonizing dullness in which stocks display a significant immunity to bad news.

CHAPTER THIRTEEN

Some Guiding Rules

Timing More Important than Issues — Never
Quarrel with the Tape—Buy or Sell "at Market"

WHEN it comes to setting down in black and white definite
rules for stock market speculation, the trouble is that the
majority of people expect a dozen or so dogmatic guides to be
promulgated. All that an experienced person can do is to offer
certain practical and fundamental observations which may help
to avoid the demonstrated, recurrent, human errors of judgment
in operations so frequently attended by emotional thinking.

It will never be possible to lay down seriatim a set of formulae
to beat the stock market any more than it will be to evolve a
method for beating Monte Carlo. Conditions are not the same
at the top of every bull market or at the bottom of every bear
swing. There have been bull markets when money commanded
a prohibitive figure and there have been bear markets when
money has been going begging, and there is yet to be devised an
infallible rule for appraising stock prices by measuring earning
power. All that anyone can do in proffering rules is to attempt
to avoid everyday errors of speculative reasoning.

In the first place, it cannot be over-emphasized that there is
no easy road to riches. A subscriber submits to *Barron's* 13
queries to encompass the problem of "What are the easiest ways
that can be used to make money in the stock market?" At the
bottom of the letter he adds that he wants those questions
answered "shortly and simply" as he hasn't "the patience to read
articles for months on end." Such an attitude is the very epitome
of wanting "something for nothing." In speculation, eternal
vigilance, which means the devotion of time and energy to the

study of values, is absolutely essential if one expects to succeed.

First question submitted by this subscriber was whether investment trust shares are not the investment solution for the average trader. The answer must necessarily be that, regardless of management, in speculating through investment trust shares one merely delegates responsibility. By so doing it is impossible to train oneself in the knowledge of the stock market and of speculative values. Investment trust losses or profits on paper multiply rapidly in the event of a sharp decline or rise in the stock market because of the big commitments. The huge blocks of stock owned by investment trusts, however, make it impossible for management of the highest order to operate with the same flexibility as can an individual.

Great doubt seems to exist in the minds of the average trader over the advisability of putting "all eggs in one basket" or resorting to diversification. The answer is that in a changing world, and especially where Government interferes with business, diversification is absolutely vital. In periods of revival or depression there is no telling where the lightning will strike. *The only way to hedge against the hazards of business fortunes is to diversify.*

Which is the more important—issue or industry? First comes the industry and then the individual stocks. Is it better to own one stock in one industry or to spread out, and how far should a diversification program be carried? *The average speculator should confine his operations to not over half-a-dozen industries and to not over a total of 15 to 20 individual issues.* In so doing he is enabled to buy two or three stocks—rather than one—in each group and to confine his operations to a number of industries that can be followed with some reasonable degree of diligence.

Now that "bigness" is arousing governmental, if not social, antagonism, the question of whether to choose a small or a large company is paramount. Here no hard and fast rule can be furnished. In industries that have reached their full stature, like steels and motors, the biggest and strongest companies are the best risks, since it is impossible for a small company to prosper rapidly where the capital investment is so large and the margin of profit promises to narrow. In the chemical and merchandising industries small companies may be all right, if the record of growth, finances and profits is convincing.

Prime management, availability of information and marketability of stock are prime attributes of a sound speculative investment. Unless these are present a stock may be subject to abnormally wide price swings characteristic of so-called specialties, and may fail to enlist the public following that makes for market leadership.

By now, however, all of these desiderata are so well recognized as to place a heavy premium on the so-called gilt-edged issues. What everybody wants tends to become scarce so that the "best issues" have for a long time sold at somewhat fantastic ratios to earnings. The danger of a somewhat artificial market status must be recognized in the event of any change in money conditions, since the big investor has come to disregard income return.

Having settled on certain fundamentals of policy, an individual should next pick out a good broker. The integrity of brokerage houses, now that balance sheet statements are available and Stock Exchange supervision constant, calls for little investigation. But it is important that a firm be chosen which has an adequate investigating department, which endeavors to present logic instead of mass reasoning as an approach to market problems, and which can demonstrate by its record of advices flexibility of judgment.

A leading financial daily, such as *The Wall Street Journal*, and/or a first-class financial weekly like *Barron's*, should provide source material for the wide-awake speculator. Only from thorough reading can a basis for sound judgment be found.

When to buy or to sell is far more important than what to buy or to sell. Briefly what that means is to satisfy one's own judgment concerning the main trend, bullish or bearish. Study of the phenomena of bull and bear markets, as outlined in preceding chapters, may be of help in arriving at a clear-cut opinion concerning which direction the market is most likely to take.

Requirements of a good trader are judgment and patience. One man may have judgment but lack staying power, while another may have patience to the point of stubbornness without the compensating quality of sound judgment. From observation and experience it may be possible gradually to compound a happy mixture of both qualities.

There is no need for one always to be in the stock market. If there are valid doubts over the main trend, it is wise to withdraw. If the market doctors disagree—if forecasters of good standing are diametrically opposed—stay on the side lines of Wall Street. Sometimes it is just as profitable to be patient in the retention of cash as in holding securities.

Fix in advance, so far as possible, a level at which to buy or to sell and stick to the figure. Carefully reasoned calculations are soundest but are likely to be distorted by the speculative atmosphere of the moment. If stock has been sold at the beginning of a bear market, pick out some level at which it is to be replaced and adhere to the initial judgment. Pursue the same tactics in locating a selling level in a bull market. Who in the brokerage business can fail to recall in roaring bull markets predictions from reliable sources that "General Motors will double," and then, when the magical figure was reached, be told that "It is still cheap?" The sequel usually was a slump.

Never challenge what has the earmarks of a reversal of the main market trend. There is a lot of hardboiled advice in *"Never quarrel with the tape."* A sharp break after a protracted, outstanding rise should never be regarded as a buying opportunity. When an initial recovery starts after a sickening liquidating movement, short sales should not be attempted merely because the market has apparently moved up too fast.

The corollary of all this is that if averaging, which is dangerous, is attempted, it should be always with instead of against the trend. Never fight a trend, so buy additionally as stocks rise and sell additionally as the market declines.

Reversal of a major movement, a rally in a bear market or a

reaction in a bull market, both of which are deceptive and difficult to analyze, on the average amounts to $33\frac{1}{3}\%$ to 50% of the first price movement. The most salient characteristic of the tapering off of a so-called "corrective movement" is dullness, at the top of a rally or the bottom of a reaction.

Sometimes propounded is the query: When is it best to buy and to sell stocks? No easy rule, as when it is safe to eat oysters, can be advanced in this respect. Statisticians have studied seasonal market movements galore only to make the worst of prognostications. Though business is most markedly subject to the seasonal influences of spring and fall buying, it by no means follows that the spring and fall are the best times to buy in good times or to sell in periods of depression. The only strongly defined seasonal movement over the years, that has held true in the vast majority of both bull and bear markets, is the January rise which begins in the latter part of December and slackens by the second week of January.

That "news favors the trend" is one of the oldest of speculative maxims. If a market is headed upward, something unexpected is constantly occurring to accelerate the advance, and vice versa in a bear market. No one ever knows whence and when an event that may transform the stock market picture will occur, though one will always hear at the bottom of a bear market "What can occur to put stocks up?" and, at the top of a bull market, "What can put the market down?" It is the unexpected that is always taking place in the market place, though what are regarded as "accidents" invariably favor the line of least resistance.

It seems that under the SEC regulations major news developments are seldom discounted in advance. Years ago the tritest of axioms was to "Sell when the good news is out." Now that insiders and manipulators, always prone to attempt to capitalize news in advance, are barred from the speculative arena, the tendency is for the market to respond to news after it is made public. But such a premise doesn't necessarily usurp the time-honored function of the stock market as a whole of interpreting the future business and profits trends of industry.

A hoary old axiom, still disregarded by the public, is "cut losses short and let profits run." What that means is quickly to abandon a position that appears to be unsound, but to retain to the very limit—through the exercise of patience—a profitable trend. The judicious use of stop orders is the best insurance against allowing losses to pile up.

Comfort oneself with the knowledge that few speculators can ever get the tops or bottoms of big market swings. Discounting errors of judgment, it is physically impossible for a big body of speculators to sell at the top and buy at the bottom for the plain reason that the market isn't big enough. Exact bottoms and tops are usually made on a minor volume of transactions. One of the biggest market operators always maintained that less than 10% of the people in the stock market ever got out in the top area.

The same operator, who naturally traded on a huge scale, always made it a practice of buying only when he could secure an important line of securities in a narrow range, say within a point or so, and to sell when the market was big enough to take big offerings in a narrow range. Following that method on a large or small scale is productive of the greatest speculative efficiency, for it simply amounts to sound merchandising—which is the essence of speculation.

In nine cases out of 10 it is best to buy or to sell "at the market." Let the broker do the best he can instead of straining for a fractional point or so of advance. Fortunes have been lost in holding out for a round price or a set profit.

Never rely too much on business men or *"insiders"*. An insider can recommend a stock, but he seldom can advise selling because of the harm it conceivably might do to his company. The average business man most of the time finds it hard to reconcile the market with his own business, and, though he has learned from experience to pay attention to sudden liquidation as a warning of bad times, he seldom has the vision to sell when the skies are clearest and to buy when the clouds are darkest. Speculators usually start the ball rolling in one direction or another and business men follow along.

Above all, read and reflect. Nothing is more vital, except good health, than the preservation of capital. The history of fortunes shows that it is more difficult to conserve than to accumulate. It will always be an ever-changing world and consequently the market will always fluctuate. Forget the present and strive to visualize what can take place three or four months hence.

CHAPTER FOURTEEN

More Rules and Some Pitfalls

AMPLIFICATION of speculative rules is bound to stress the essentially speculative character of common stocks. A fundamental attribute of a good investment is that it should be a good speculation. And where speculation exists, risk is present. Something can be said for the old bucketshop philosophy "stocks were meant to be sold." Coming down to brass tacks, stocks should never be put away for an indefinite hold.

Because salability is greatest on the New York Stock Exchange, by and large, issues chosen by an investor-speculator should enjoy the Exchange listing. In addition to the advantage of salability is the fact that any change for better or worse soon shows up on the ticker tape which affords the proverbial "goldfish" privacy with respect to corporate developments. Any turn is dramatically reflected in glaring price changes that can be readily observed and appraised.

In choosing stocks listed on the Stock Exchange, "seasoning" is desirable. Several market panics and business depressions are what try the mettle of a company. A record in bad times as well as in good is needed to determine the nature of earnings achievements.

Stress has already been laid on the manner in which fashions in the stock market change. There are, however, certain industries that, because of their "in-and-out" record, are almost permanently out of fashion. Some, like steel and railroad equipments, are in the "prince and pauper" class, while others have for so long a period enjoyed so transient a prosperity as to fall into the discard. In this hapless group are sugars, textiles, leathers and packers.

In approaching the problems of investment it must again be reiterated that an independent point of view is that which alone can, through trial and error and the testing of experience, inculcate needed self-reliance. Remarks of politicians, statesmen, bankers and business men should, for the most part, be taken with a grain of salt. Too imbued with present conditions are most public utterances to represent clear-sighted analysis of the future.

Following are two old homilies which bewildered market followers may treat with a healthy skepticism. "Never sell America short," attributed to the elder J. P. Morgan, has led many an American to carry indefinitely stocks that the most superficial analysis would have shown to have deteriorated. "Common stocks as long-term investments" is a latter-day thesis that has also led many to financial ruin.

Guard against the speculative moods prevalent at the tops and bottoms of cyclical business activity. Perspective is what must be acquired. The pressure of present-day events and the psychology of the moment in tending to distort a sober, long-range view prevent unemotional analysis. It is not when the motor and steel industries are booming that the United States Steel Corp. and General Motors Corp. should be regarded as investments. And not when the steel industry is barely moving and the motor industry struggling to sell cars are United States Steel and General Motors "pure gambles."

Never put a halo around a stock—American Telephone, General Electric or whatever is the favorite of the moment. Conditions change and the stock that promised to be the prop may be the tragedy of an old age. Against too great a reliance on or too ponderous an investment in a single issue *diversification* has proved the best insurance to date.

No hard and fast rule, certainly no chart prognostication, or, in fact, no mathematical formula, is an Aladdin's lamp in Wall Street. There is hardly a time when chart theorists do not disagree on the interpretation of so-called intermediate trends.

Preoccupation with short swings can divert attention from the main trend, so disregard short swings for fear of losing main trend position.

It is also well to be on guard against too frequent switching. Switching from one stock to another, if a strong movement is under way, is rarely profitable and opens the way for two possible errors, viz., selling and buying the wrong stocks and at the wrong time. As all stocks do not move together, impatience over the apparent backwardness of an issue is what causes so much inopportune jumping in and out.

Stick to stocks concerning which you know most or where information is most readily available. "Far fields look the greenest," and the temptation to speculate on the unknown is insidious. Patience and judgment with respect to stocks carefully chosen should, in the long run, yield greater profit than what may be garnered from transitory movements.

Beware of greed and envy. Both have proved the undoing of otherwise reasonable individuals. Though the story of how much this or that person made is bound to be jarring, the chances are that such stories of quick riches have been greatly exaggerated. To keep one's balance when the market is boiling just remember how long it takes to increase capital by the simple law of interest.

Excited markets should always intensify the decision to act. After a long decline or protracted rise it is usually the wisest policy to turn quickly with the change of tide.

Worst of speculative human traits is an exaggerated ego, and the worst of all egos is pride of judgment in the stock market. Don't quarrel with the tape. Try to remain deaf to the clamor of the marketplace. Exercise prompt, firm judgment, and, trite as it may sound, aim to sell only when business is booming and to buy when the low level of business indexes is everyday gossip.

The stock market has no past. It lives for the future only. Previous prices count for nothing. The investments of today may be the trash of tomorrow, and the gambles of today may be the investments of a few years hence. Hence, always try to look ahead.

Reflecting the judgments and decisions of thousands of individuals and institutions, the stock market is in a position to see all, to hear all, and, generally, to know all. Sometimes, as in 1929, it is slow to register a forthcoming earthquake. In 1937 it was tardy in discerning a recurrence of the 1919 inventory problem. But if it holds its ground against a torrent of bad news or refuses to respond to myriad favorable developments, then it has a message which though difficult to understand at the moment will later on be clear to all.

During the World War the stock market, as the German successes on the Marne multiplied, refused to give ground, implying that Allied successes were to be the aftermath. The Bank Holidays of 1933, the market showed, were not a prelude to chaos, but the beginnings of a new business revival. The break in the spring of 1937, in the face of the most brilliant earnings and business news, was the forerunner of the disastrous 1937-'38 deflation. And the stubborn strength of equities in the spring of 1938, notwithstanding a virtual collapse of business activity and of earning power, heralded an upturn in commodities and in business.

Know as much as possible about the stocks you own. Now that manipulation is banned and stocks cannot be artificially carried to absurd extremes, apply mathematics to your speculation. Recognize that a $2 move from a $10 level, or a 20% fluctuation, is the equivalent of 20 points for a $100 stock. In the long run the laws of mathematics can be no more safely defied than the laws of interest in the stock market.

Study the performance of individual stocks. A better or worse than average appreciation or loss during a well-defined trend for some months should prompt fresh investigation, and, though switching is to be avoided as far as possible, there is no point in staying with a lost cause. Persistent investigation may uncover subsurface developments that the market has been measuring.

Never let stocks run over 10% against you. As that used to be the old-time margin, to allow a loss of over 10% to pile up is to disregard the cynical axiom of "sell on the first margin call." If the market has proved your judgment wrong, admit the error promptly.

Never speculate for a specific financial need. To do so is to act impulsively—to "press", as golfers would have it. The motivation in such circumstances will be emotional, with the twin elements of patience and judgment conspicuously lacking. In 99 cases out of 100 the timing will be wrong.

The stock market can do anything. It can rise on what appears to be the most discouraging news and it can fall on what purport to be the most stimulating developments. Its perversity in this respect is simply born of its disregard of the momentary and its recognition of the far future.

What is true of the market has virtually become true of economics. The most cherished tenets of that science have been shattered in the past few years. In *The New Republic* of Sept. 15, 1937, Chester T. Crowell, who counts himself a practical economist for a quarter of a century, pokes fun at "The Learned Economists." Twenty years ago the economist knew "positively that there was no such thing as going off the gold standard," and, the author goes on to say, "at present most of the nations of the earth are off the gold standard. And virtually all of the recovery from the depression is taking place in those nations." Italy, it was declared, couldn't carry on an Ethiopian war with a $300,000,000 gold reserve, and yet it succeeded. He says further, "At this moment Russia is the second gold-producing country of the globe. And Russia doesn't believe in gold." It may help in the whirligig of the New Deal to dwell on one of his sentences: "In economics we are beginning again from scratch." In other words, economics, as well as the stock market is no longer susceptible to old-fashioned, hard-and-fast conclusions.

Thus openmindedness and flexibility of judgment are what are needed to produce successful results in a market where the unexpected can always happen. While study and reflection should be taking place all the time, act one must, and quickly, when the time comes. Thousands of other people are pitting their judgment against yours. If opportunity is knocking, one can be sure that plenty of individuals are listening. No engraved invitations or specific dates for buying and selling are ever sent out from Wall Street.

Never forget that all market profits are "paper" until collected. A $1,000 or $100,000 paper profit can soon turn into a loss from mental lethargy or indecision.

Inasmuch as 99% of speculators trade on the bull side, *get out somewhere while the going is good.* For most people a bull market is like a trip in an elevator. Floor after floor is called out by the starter, but few emerge. Finally, to continue the metaphor, the elevator reaches the roof as the bull market is culminating. Then the machinery breaks, the car plunges to the bottom of the shaft, and the passengers—most of them badly injured—struggle to climb out of the wreckage that a bear market has brought.